D1543000

THE HOME UNIVERSITY LIBRARY
OF MODERN KNOWLEDGE

42

ROME

The Editors of the *Home University Library*
since its foundation in 1911 have included

GILBERT MURRAY, O.M., F.B.A.

THE RT. HON. H. A. L. FISHER, O.M., F.R.S.

SIR ARTHUR THOMSON

SIR JULIAN HUXLEY, F.R.S.

SIR GEORGE CLARK, F.B.A.

SIR HENRY TIZARD, F.R.S.

AND

SIR GAVIN DE BEER, F.R.S.

The present Editors are

MICHAEL ABERCROMBIE, F.R.S.

AND

A. D. WOOZLEY

R O M E

W. WARDE FOWLER

Revised by

M. P. CHARLESWORTH

Second Edition

LONDON
OXFORD UNIVERSITY PRESS
NEW YORK   TORONTO

Oxford University Press, Amen House, London E.C.4

GLASGOW NEW YORK TORONTO MELBOURNE WELLINGTON
BOMBAY CALCUTTA MADRAS KARACHI LAHORE DACCA
CAPE TOWN SALISBURY NAIROBI IBADAN ACCRA
KUALA LUMPUR HONG KONG

First published in 1912, *and reprinted in* 1917, 1919, 1921,
1923, 1925, 1926, 1927, 1928, 1932, 1935 *and* 1939.
Second Edition 1947, *reprinted in* 1949, 1952, 1957, 1960
and 1965

Street
2958
.3495
.11

PRINTED IN GREAT BRITAIN

PREFACE TO THE SECOND EDITION

WARDE FOWLER'S *Rome*, first published in 1912, is such a little classic in itself that I have not attempted to make any alterations save in those places where statements of fact needed modification in the light of newer knowledge, or where certain topical allusions would now seem out of date. But I have revised the Bibliography by including in it some English books which have appeared since Warde Fowler wrote, and which are not too bulky or too technical. I hope that in its revised form the book may still represent the wise and understanding interpretation that a great scholar has given of Roman history and of the Roman character.

M. P. C.

St. John's College, Cambridge
1947

CONTENTS

	PREFACE TO THE SECOND EDITION	.	.	5
I.	INTRODUCTORY	.	.	.	.	.	7
II.	THE ADVANCE OF ROME IN ITALY	.	.	20
III.	THE TRAINING OF THE ROMAN CHARACTER	37
IV.	THE STRUGGLE WITH CARTHAGE AND HANNIBAL	.	.	.	.	.	56
V.	DOMINION AND DEGENERACY	.	.	.	73
VI.	THE REVOLUTION: ACT I	.	.	.	89
VII.	THE REVOLUTION: ACT II	.	.	.	105
VIII.	AUGUSTUS—THE REVIVAL OF THE ROMAN SPIRIT	.	.	.	.	.	.	122
IX.	LIFE IN THE ROMAN EMPIRE	.	.	.	138
X.	THE EMPIRE UNDER THE ANTONINES— CONCLUSION	.	.	.	.	149
	BIBLIOGRAPHY	.	.	.	.	.	165
	INDEX	.	.	.	.	.	.	167

CHAPTER I

INTRODUCTORY

LET us suppose an ordinary Englishman, with no special knowledge of classical history, to be looking at a collection of Roman antiquities in the cases of a museum. He will probably not linger long over these cases, but will pass on to something more likely to attract his interest. The objects he is looking at are, for the most part, neither striking nor beautiful, and the same are presented for his inspection over and over again as collections from various Roman sites. They are chiefly useful things, implements and utensils of all kinds, and fragments of military weapons and armour. In the coins he can take no delight, because, apart from the fact that, uninterpreted, they have no tale to tell him, they do not excite his admiration by beauty of design and workmanship. If, indeed, he were visiting a museum at Rome, he would find plenty of beautiful things in it; but these are works of Greek artists, imported by wealthy or tasteful Romans in the later ages of Rome's history. A typical collection of genuine Roman antiquities would probably have the effect I describe. Utility, not beauty, would seem to have been the motive of the people who left these things behind them.

The same motive will also be suggested to us if we visit any of the larger Roman works either in this country or on the Continent. Most of us know the look of a Roman road running straight over hill and valley, and meant mainly for military purposes, to enable troops to move rapidly and to survey the country as they marched. In the towns which have been excavated, we usually find that the most spacious and striking buildings must have been the meeting-halls (*basilicae*), in which business of all kinds was transacted, and especially business connected with law and government. Very often, though not in the comparatively poor province of Britain, this character-istic of utility is combined with another—solidity and imposing size. In this well-watered island the Romans did not need aqueducts to bring a constant supply of water to their towns, but in Italy and the south of France these great works are sometimes unnecessarily huge and imposing. Even when they left the path of strict utility, as in their triumphal arches and gate-ways, for which we must go to Trier in Germany, or to Orange in the south of France, or to Italy itself, they held strongly to the principles of solidity and imposing size. A writer who knew their art well has said that their notion of the highest of all things, their *summum bonum*, was not the beautiful, but the powerful, and that they thought they had as a people received this notion from heaven.

It would, indeed, be wrong to say that there is no beauty in Roman art; but it is quite in accordance with what has just been said, that even in the best of it there is a strong tendency to realism, to matter of fact. In their sculpture they were especially strong in portraiture, and in depicting scenes of human life they never or rarely idealize. A battle scene, or a picture on stone of life in a city, is crowded with figures, just because it really was so, and the work is without that restfulness for the eye which the perfect grouping of a Greek artist so often supplies. So, too, in literature; all their greatest poetry has a strictly practical object, and bears directly on human life. The great philosophical poem of Lucretius was meant to rescue the Romans from religious superstition; the object of the *Aeneid* of Virgil, of which I shall have more to say in another chapter, was to recall the degenerate Roman of that day to the sense of duty in the home and in the State. Their one original invention in literary form was satire, by which they meant comment, friendly or hostile, on the human life around them. Their myths and legends, of which there was no such abundant crop as in Greece, dealt chiefly with the founding of cities, or with the heroic deeds of human beings.[1] On the whole they excelled most in oratory and history; and their prose came to perfection earlier than their poetry.

One other feature of their character shall be mentioned here, which is entirely in keeping with the rest, and often escapes notice. If in the works of their hands and their brains they were not an imaginative people, we can well understand that they had not this gift in practical life. Imagination in action takes the form of adventurousness, as we may see in our own history; the literary imaginativeness of Elizabethan England has its counterpart in the adventurous voyages of Elizabethan seamen. The Romans were not an adventurous people; they were not imaginative enough to be so. They penetrated, indeed, into unknown countries; Caesar reached Britain and bridged the Rhine, but that great man, a true Roman born, had a temperament rather scientific than romantic. He did as almost all conquering Romans had done before him, and were to do after him—he advanced solidly, making his way safe behind him and feeling carefully in front of him. His book about his wars in Gaul was written

---

[1] The best known of these, and perhaps the most beautiful, is that of Coriolanus, which has descended from Plutarch to Shakespeare, and so become immortal.

without a touch of imagination, and for strictly practical purposes. There is, indeed, in the generation before Caesar, an exception so striking that it may be said to prove the rule; he who reads Plutarch's charming life of Sertorius, an Italian from the mountains of central Italy, will find both romance and adventure in his story.

It is plain, then, that we have to do in this volume with a people not of imagination, but of action: a people intensely alive to the necessities and difficulties of human life. The Romans were, in fact, the most practical people in history; and this enabled them to supply what was wanting to the civilization of the Mediterranean basin in the work of the Greeks. They themselves were well aware of this quality, and proud of it. We find it expressed by the elder Cato quite at the beginning of the best age of Roman literature; his ideal Roman is *vir fortis et strenuus*—a man of strong courage and active energy. Tacitus, in the later days of that literature, says that all designs and deeds should be directed to the practical ends of life (*ad utilitatem vitae*). Midway between these two, we have the great Latin poets constantly singing of the hardihood and the practical virtues which had made Rome great, and Italy great under Rome's leadership. 'A race of hardy breed, we carry our children to the streams and harden them in the bitter, icy water; as boys they spend wakeful nights over the chase, and tire out the woodland, but in manhood, unwearied by toil and trained to poverty, they subdue the soil with their mattocks, or shake towns in war' (Virgil, *Aen.* ix, 607 foll.). These lines, though applied to an Italian stock, were meant to remind the Roman of a life that had once been his. The words in which the Romans delighted as expressing their national char-

acteristics, all tell the same tale: *gravitas*, the serious-
ness of demeanour which is the outward token of a
steadfast purpose; *continentia*, self-restraint; *industria*
and *diligentia*, words which we have inherited from
them, needing no explanation; *constantia*, perseverance
in conduct; and last, not least, *virtus*, manliness, which
originally meant activity and courage, and with ripening
civilization took on a broader and more ethical meaning.
Quotations might be multiplied a thousandfold to
prove the honest admiration of this people for their
own nobler qualities. As exemplified in an individual,
Plutarch's life of the elder Cato, which can be read
as well in English as in the original Greek, will give a
good idea of these.

But it is essential to note that this hard and practical
turn of the Roman mind was in some ways curiously
limited. It cannot be said that they excelled either in
industrial or commercial pursuits. Agriculture was
their original occupation, and trade-gilds existed at
Rome very early in her history; but the story of their
agriculture is rather a sad one, and Rome has never
become a great industrial city. For the scientific
practice of husbandry they turned to a translation from
the Carthaginian, and their methods of commerce they
learnt chiefly from the Greeks. It was in another
direction that their genius for practical work drew
them: to the arts and methods of discipline, law,
government.

We can see this peculiar gift showing itself at all
stages of their development: in the agricultural family
which was the germ of all their later growth, in the
city-state which grew from that germ, and in the
Empire, founded by the leaders of the city-state, and
organized by Augustus and his successors. It is seen,
too, in their military system, which won them their

empire; they did not fight merely for spoil or glory, but for clearly realized practical purposes. As Tacitus says of a single German tribe which possessed something of this gift, the Romans did not so much go out to battle as to war. True, they constantly made blunders and suffered defeat; they often 'muddled through' difficulties as we do ourselves; but they refused to recognize defeat, and profited by adverse fortune. Listen once more to a few words of old Cato; in his *Origins of Rome*, written for his son, he wrote: 'Adversity tames us, and teaches us our true line of conduct, while good fortune is apt to warp us from the way of prudence.' Thus they went on from defeat to victory, conquest and government. It is worth while not only to lay to heart, but to learn by heart, the famous lines in which Virgil sums up the Roman's conception of his own work in the world—

Others will mould their bronzes to breathe with a tenderer
    grace,
Draw, I doubt not, from marble a vivid life to the face,
Plead at the bar more deftly, with sapient wands of the wise
Trace heaven's courses and changes, predict us stars to arise.
Thine, O Roman, remember, to reign over every race!
These be thine arts, thy glories, the ways of peace to proclaim,
Mercy to show to the fallen, the proud with battle to tame!
    Aeneid, vi, 847–853 (Bowen's translation).

It was this power of ruling, which itself implies a habit of discipline, that marked out Rome as the natural successor of Greece in European civilization; and it grew naturally out of the purely practical bent of the early Romans, who were unhampered in their constant activity by fancy, reflection, or culture. Without it, we may doubt if the work of the Greeks would have been saved for us when the storms from the north, invasions of barbarian peoples, fell at last upon the sunny lands filled with the spirit of Greek thought and the divine works of Greek artists. To Roman discipline, law, and government, we owe not only much that even now is every day of practical benefit to us, but the preservation of what we still possess of the treasures of Hellenic genius.

For this reason I assume that this book will be taken up by most readers after they have made some acquaintance with the history and thought of the Greeks. It is true that the history of the two peoples is best looked at as one great whole; there is a general likeness in their institutions; the form of the State, and the ideas of government, with which each grew to maturity, were in the main the same. But Roman mental development was much slower than Greek; and Greece was already beginning to lose her vitality when Rome was still illiterate and unable to record her own history adequately. Thus Greek influence was the first to tell upon the world; the basin of the Mediterranean was already permeated by the Greek spirit when Roman influence began to work upon it; and there can be no doubt that he who begins with Roman history and then goes on to Greek is reversing the natural order of things.

I will also assume that those who have begun to read this book are provided with some knowledge of that Mediterranean basin which is the scene of Graeco-Roman history; such as can be gained by frequent contemplation of a good map. They will be familiar with Sicily and south Italy, which were teeming with Greek settlements when Roman history really begins. They will probably have realized how short a step it is from Italy to Africa, whether or no Sicily be taken as a stepping-stone; Cato could show fresh figs in the Roman senate which had been grown in Carthaginian territory. They will have realized that you can pass from the 'heel' of Italy to the Hellenic peninsula in a single night, as Caesar did when he embarked his army at Brindisi to attack his rival; such geographical facts are of immense importance in explaining not only the foreign policy of Rome, but also the development of her culture. And thus furnished, they will begin to be curious about the destiny of the Italian peninsula, of which Greek history has had little to tell them. Leaving that question for the present, they will wish to know why the Greeks did not colonize the centre and north of Italy as they did the south and south-west, but left room enough for a new type of civilization to grow up there. And above all, they will wish to know how and why a single city on the western coast should have succeeded in building up a great power in Italy quite independent of Greece, and destined eventually to supersede her, which may be reckoned as a factor almost as important in the making of our modern civilization as Hellas herself.

This last question is the one which I must try to answer in the earlier part of this book; in the later chapters I shall have to deal with another one—how this single city-state contrived to weld together the whole Mediterranean civilization, strongly enough to give it several centuries of security against uncivilized enemies in the north, and half-civilized enemies in the east. But for the moment let us see why the Greeks did not permeate Italy with their own civilization as they did Sicily: how it was that they left room for a new power, capable eventually of shielding them and their work from destruction. To answer this question we must consider the nature of the Italian peninsula, and the character of the races then living in it.

The simple fact is that though the shrewd commercial Greek had seized on all the best harbours in the long, narrow peninsula, these harbours were all on the south coast, about the 'heel' of Italy, or on the south-west coast in the volcanic region of the modern Naples, which was itself one of these Greek settlements. The east coast north of the 'heel' is almost harbourless, as will be realized by any one who takes the route by rail to Brindisi on his way to Egypt or India. *Italy is a mountainous country*—a fact never to be forgotten in Roman history—and its mountains, the long chain of the Apennines, have their spinal ridge much nearer the east than the west coast, and descend upon the sea so sharply on that side that for long distances road or railway only just finds a passage. All along this east coast there was nothing to tempt Greeks to settle, and as they rarely or never penetrated far inland from their settlements, their influence never spread into this mountainous region from the many sea-coast towns of Magna Graecia, as their part of Italy was called. On the Bay of Naples they had, indeed, a better chance; here there was a rich fertile plain stretching away to the hills, which on this side come down less steeply than on the eastern; this we shall hear of again as the Plain of Campania, in which Greek influence was very strong and active, capable of penetrating beyond its limits northward. But north of this again they left no permanent settlements; good harbours are wanting, and such as there are were occupied about the eighth century B.C. by a people at that time as enterprising as themselves, the Etruscans. These, too, had been recent immigrants into the peninsula from the east, and together with the Greeks they formed the only obstacles to the growth of a native Italian power—a power, that is, belonging to the older races that had long been settled there. The Greeks were not likely to interfere with such a growth, as we have seen; whether the Etruscans were to do so we have yet to see.

It was, in fact, this Etruscan people who first gave an Italian stock the chance of rising into a great Mediterranean power; and in order to understand how this was, we must look at a good map of central Italy, which gives a fair idea of the elevations in this part of the peninsula. Looking at such a map, it is easy to see that the long, narrow leg of Italy is cloven in twain about the middle by a river, the Tiber, the only river of considerable size and real historical importance, south of the Po. It is formed of several streams which descend from the central mass of the Apennines, now called the Abruzzi, but soon gathers into a swift though not a wide river, and emerges from that mountainous district some five-and-twenty miles from the sea, into what we now call the Roman Campagna, the Latium of ancient times; skirting the northern edge of this comparatively level district it falls into the sea, without forming a natural harbour, about half-way up the western coast of the peninsula. To the north of it and of the plain were settled a number of cities, more or less independent of each other, forming the Etruscan people, whose origin we do not yet know for certain, and whose language has never been deciphered from the inscriptions they have left behind them; a mysterious race, active in war and commerce, who had subdued but not exterminated the native population around them. To the east and south of the Tiber, stretching far along the mountainous region and its western out-skirts, was a race of hardy mountaineers, broken up, as hill peoples usually are, into a number of com-munities without any principle of cohesion except that of the various tribes to which they belonged. The northern part of this sturdy hill-folk was known as

Umbrians and Sabines; the southern part as Samnites or Oscans. They all spoke dialects of the same tongue, a tongue akin to those which most European peoples still speak. Lastly, immediately to the south of the Tiber in the last part of its course, occupying the plain which stretches here between the mountains, the river, and the sea, there was settled another branch of this same stock, speaking another dialect destined to be known for ever as Latin. These three sub-races of a great stock—Umbrians, Samnites, and Latins—are meant when we speak of a native Italian population as opposed to Greek or Etruscan immigrants. Doubtless they were not the aboriginal inhabitants of the country, but of older stocks history knows nothing that concerns us in this book. These are the peoples who were destined to be supreme in the Mediterranean basin, and eventually to govern the whole civilized world.

It is as well to be quite clear at once that the acquisition of this supremacy was not the work of one only of these peoples, the Latins, or of one city only of the Latins, i.e. Rome. It was the work of all these stocks which I have called native Italian. Roman is a convenient word, and Rome was all along the leader in action and the organizing power; but the material, and in a great part as time went on the brain-power also, was contributed by all these peoples taken together. They had first to submit to the great leader and organizer, Rome, a fate against which, as we shall see, they struggled long; but no sooner had they submitted than they were added to the account of Italian development, and with few exceptions played their new part with a good courage.

So much, then, for the Italian peoples who were to supersede the Greeks in the world's history. But let us now return for a moment to the Tiber, and fix our eyes on the last five-and-twenty miles of its course, where it separates the plain of Latium from the Etruscan people to the north. The Latin-speaking stock were far more in danger from these Etruscans than the Umbrian and Samnite mountaineers; nothing but the river was between them and their enemies, for enemies they undoubtedly were, bent on pushing farther south, like the Danes in England in the ninth century of our era. The Latins had, indeed, a magnificent natural fortress in the middle of their plain, in the extinct volcano of the Alban mountain, some 3,000 feet above sea-level; and here, according to a sure tradition, was their original chief city, Alba Longa. But this was of no avail against an invader from the north; it was the river that was the vital concern of Latium when once the Etruscans had become established to the north of it. Now at one point, some twenty miles by water from the river's mouth, was a group of small hills, rising to a height of about 160 feet, three of them almost isolated and abutting on the stream, and the others in reality a part of the plain to the south, with their northern sides falling somewhat steeply towards the Tiber. Here, too, was an island in the river, which might give an enemy an easy chance of crossing. On this position there arose at some uncertain date, but beyond doubt as a fortress against the Etruscan power, a city called *Roma*; and there a city has been ever since, known by the same name. It is likely enough that it was an outpost founded by the city of Alba Longa, which eventually itself vanished out of history; and this was the tradition of later days. If we can accept the motive of the foundation—the defence of Latium against her foe—we need not trouble about the many legends of it.

Rome started on her wonderful career as a military

outpost of a people akin to her, and face to face with an enemy with whom she had no sort of relationship. If she could but hold her position there was obviously a great future for her. The position on the Tiber was, in fact, strategically the best in Italy. It is, as a great Roman historian said, just in the centre of the peninsula. There was easy access to the sea both by land and water, and a way open into central Italy up the Tiber valley—the one great natural entrance from the sea. She was far enough from the sea to be safe from raiders, yet near enough to be in communication with other peoples by means of shipping. If enemies attacked her from different directions inland, she could move against them on what in military language we may call 'inner lines'—she could strike simultaneously from a common base. From the sea no power dared attack her, until in her degenerate days Gaiseric landed at Ostia in A.D. 455. On the whole we may say that no other city in Italy had the same chance, as regards position, of dominating the whole of Italy, and that in those early days of her history the Etruscans unwittingly taught her how to use this great advantage. Just as the kingdom of the West Saxons, and their supremacy in England, was built up by the stern necessity of having to resist the Danes, so the Romans became a leading people in Italy by virtue of having to withstand the Etruscans.

In my next chapter I propose to tell the story in outline (and in detail it cannot be told for want of knowledge) of the advance of the Roman power to the leadership of Italy. Then I will try and explain the qualities and the organization which enabled her to turn her chances to account.

CHAPTER II

THE ADVANCE OF ROME IN ITALY

I SAID in the last chapter that if Rome could only hold the line of the lower Tiber against the Etruscans, great possibilities of advance were open to her. How long she held it we do not know; but there is hardly a doubt that in course of time—some time probably in the sixth century B.C.—she lost it, and even herself fell into the hands of the enemy. The tale is not told in her legendary annals; but we have other convincing evidence. The last three kings of Rome seem to have been Etruscans. The great temple of Jupiter on the Capitoline hill, which was founded at this time, was in the Etruscan style, and built on foundations of Etruscan masonry, some of which can still be seen. Below this temple, as you go to the river, was a street called the street of the Etruscans, and there are other signs of the conquest which need not be given here. On the whole we may believe that this persistent enemy crossed the Tiber higher up, where she already had a footing, and so took the city in flank and rear.

Fortunately, the Etruscans were not in the habit of destroying the cities they took: they occupied and made use of them. They seem to have used Rome to spread their influence over Latium: they built a temple of Jupiter on the Alban hill, the old centre of a Latin league: and there is strong evidence that they made Rome the head of another and later league, with a religious centre in a temple of Diana, who was not originally a Roman deity, on the Aventine hill overlooking the Tiber. All events in this Etruscan period are very dim and doubtful, but it looks as if the very loss of the line of defence had only given the conquered city a new lease of life, with a widened outlook and fresh opportunities. But was she to continue as an Etruscan city? The question reminds us of a crisis in our own history: was England to become a Norman-French country after the Conquest?

At this time it seems that the Etruscans were being harassed from the north by Gallic tribes, who had already spread over north-west Europe, and were conquering the valley of the Po and pressing farther south. This may account for the undoubted fact that about the end of the sixth century B.C. Rome did succeed in throwing off the Etruscan yoke: that the old Roman families united to expel their foreign king, and to establish an aristocratic republic. Henceforward the very name of king (*rex*) was held in abhorrence by the Romans, and the government passed into the hands of two yearly elected magistrates, with absolute power as leaders in war, and a limited power within the city. In the next chapter I will explain this new form of government more fully: here it will be enough to say that they were called consuls, and that they had an advising body (as the kings probably had before them) of the heads of noble families, called *senatus*, or a body of elderly men. At present let us go on with the story of Rome's advance in Italy.

According to the legend, the Etruscans made a vigorous attempt to recover Rome. This is a picturesque story, and is admirably told in one of Macaulay's famous *Lays of Ancient Rome*. But we must pass it over here, for we have no means of testing the truth of it. Soon afterwards we come upon what seems to be a real historical fact, a treaty between Rome and the other Latin cities, the text of which was preserved for many centuries. This treaty shows plainly that henceforward we have to reckon Rome and Latium as one power in Italy; and this is the first real forward step in the advance of Rome. It guaranteed in the first place mutual support in war; Rome needed support against the Etruscans, and the Latin cities at the southern end of the plain were liable to be attacked by hill tribes from the east and south. Still more important as showing the advance of civilization was the sanction of a common system of private law. Any citizen of a Latin city (including, of course, Rome) was to be able to buy and sell, to hold and inherit property, in any other city, in full confidence that he would be protected by the law of that city in so doing; and if he married a woman of another city his marriage was legitimate and his children could inherit his property according to law.[1] This was going a long way towards making a single state of the whole of Latium. All the communities were on equal terms, and all had certain legal relations with each other; and these are two of the chief features of a true federation. Now all federations were an improvement on the isolation of the single city-state, which was helpless in those days of turbulence and invasion. This one looks like the work of a statesman; and if that statesman was a Roman, Spurius Cassius, as tradition asserted, then Rome had achieved her first victory in the arts of statesmanship and diplomacy with which she was destined to rule the world.

Before we go on with our story let us notice how well Latium was geographically fitted to develop a federation, as compared with the more mountainous districts of Italy. Latium was a plain, as its name

---

[1] The Latin words which expressed these two mutual rights, *commercium* and *connubium*, are still in use in various forms in the languages of modern Europe.

seems to imply; and like Boeotia in Greece it was naturally suited for federative union, while tribes living in the highlands always found it difficult to unite. Again, the Latins were jammed into a comparatively small space between the hills and the sea, and their strength was concentrated by their position: while the Etruscans, and the various Italian stocks, were continually moving onward to look for better quarters, and losing their strength and their cohesion in doing so.

In these early federations of cities there was always a tendency for one particular city to slip into the position of leader, just as in modern federations, that of Switzerland for example, there is a continual tendency for the central authority to extend its influence. In Latium there can be no doubt that Rome very soon began to assume some kind of headship. Her position on the Tiber, and the constant strain that she had to undergo in resisting the Etruscans, gave her an advantage over the other Latin cities, who had to resist less constant annoyance from less highly civilized enemies. I mean that the Roman people had both nerve and brain so continually exercised that they developed not only brute courage, but endurance, diplomatic skill and forethought. For a whole century after they expelled their Etruscan kings they had to keep up a continual struggle with the great Etruscan city of Veii, which was only a few miles to the north of the river, on very high ground, and with the smaller town of Fidenae on the Tiber above Rome, which the Veians could make use of to attack them from that side. No wonder that when at last they succeeded in taking Veii they burnt it to the ground. It is said that they thought of migrating to that lofty site themselves, and abandoning the position on the Tiber; but they wisely gave up the idea, and Veii was sacked and her goddess Juno brought to Rome. The site is a deserted spot at the present day.

It was this prolonged struggle, in which the Latins were of course called upon to help, that placed Rome in the position of leader of the league, and from the moment it was over we find her attitude towards the Latins a changed one. It is likely enough that she had long been growing overbearing and unpopular with the other cities, but of this, if it was so, we have no certain details. What we do know is that at the beginning of the fourth century B.C., when a terrible disaster overtook Rome, the Latins failed to serve her.

This disaster was the capture and sack of Rome by a wandering tribe of Gauls from the north, who descended the valley of the Tiber, took the Romans by surprise, and utterly routed them at the little river Allia, twelve miles from the city. These Gauls were formidable in battle and fairly frightened the Romans; but, like other Celtic peoples, they were incapable of settling down into a solid State, or of making good use of their victories. They vanished as quickly as they had come, and left nothing behind them but an indelible memory of the terror they had inspired, and many stories of the agony of that catastrophe. The most characteristic of these shows the veneration of the Romans for what was perhaps their greatest political institution, the Senate. The citizens had fled to the Capitol, where they contrived to hold out till relief came; but meanwhile the older Senators, men who were past the age of fighting, determined to meet their death, and devoted themselves, according to an old religious practice resorted to in extreme peril, to the infernal deities. Each then took his seat in state robes at the door of his house. There the Gauls found them and marvelled, taking them for more than human. At last a Gaul ventured to stroke the beard of one of them named Papirius, who immediately struck him with his ivory wand: he was instantly slain, and of the rest not one survived. We need not ask whether this story is true or not, for it is impossible to test it: but it is truly Roman in feeling, and from a religious point of view it falls in line with others that were told of the sacrifice of the individual for the State.

This experience was a terrible discipline for the Romans, but no sooner had the Gauls departed than they began to turn it to practical account. They saw that they must secure the country to the north of them more effectually, and they did so by making large portions of it Roman territory, and by establishing two colonies there, i.e. garrisoned fortresses on military roads. Then they turned to deal with their own confederates, who perhaps had felt a secret satisfaction in the humiliation of a leader of whom they were jealous, and were now, especially the two great neighbouring cities of Tibur and Praeneste (Tivoli and Palestrina), beginning to rise in open revolt. Knowing what happened afterwards, we can say that these Latin cities were standing in the way of Italian progress: but to the ancient city-state independence was the very salt of life.

All public records and materials for history, except those engraved on stone, were probably destroyed in the capture and burning of Rome by the Gauls; up to this time Roman 'history' is not really worthy of the name. But from this time onward certain official records were preserved, and we gradually pass into an age which may truly be called historical. In detail it will still be questionable, chiefly owing to the tendency of Roman leading families to glorify the deeds of their own

ancestors at the expense of truth, and so to hand on
false accounts to the age when history first came to be
written down. But in the fourth and third centuries
B.C. it becomes fairly clear in outline. I said in the
last chapter that the Romans were curiously destitute
of the imaginative faculty. But no people is entirely
without imagination, and it is most interesting to find
the Romans using their moderate allowance in invent-
ing the details of noble deeds and honourable services
to the State. Provoking as it is to us, and provoking
even to the Roman historian Livy himself, who was
well aware of it, this habit has its own value as a feature
of old Roman life and character.

But I must return to the story of the advance of
Rome in Italy. It seems clear that after the Gallic
invasion the Latins became more and more discontented with Roman policy, which probably aimed
at utilizing all the resources of the league, and at the
same time getting complete control of its relations with
other powers. We have the text in Greek, preserved
by the historian Polybius, of a treaty with Carthage,
then the greatest naval power in the Mediterranean,
which well illustrates this: the date is 348 B.C. Rome
acts for Latium in negotiating this treaty; and Carthage
undertook not to molest the Latin cities, *provided that
they remained faithful to Rome*; nay, even to restore
to the power of the leading city any rebellious Latin
community that might fall into their hands. This
plainly shows that revolt was expected, and a few
years later it became general. But in spite of the
support of the Campanians in the rich volcanic plain
farther south, and indeed of danger so great that it
gave rise to another story of the '*devotio*' of a Roman
consul to the infernal deities on behalf of the State,
the Latins were completely beaten at the battle of

Mount Vesuvius, and the Romans were able so to alter the league as to deprive it of all real claim to be called a federation.

We saw that any citizen of a Latin city could buy and hold property, marry and have legitimate children, in any other Latin city, knowing that he was protected by the law in the enjoyment of these rights. But after the rebellion this was all changed. A citizen could enjoy these rights in his own city, or at Rome, but nowhere else, while a Roman could enjoy them everywhere. A citizen of Praeneste, for example, could enjoy them at Praeneste or Rome, but not in the neighbouring cities of Tibur or Tusculum: while a Roman could do business in all these cities, and be supported in all his dealings by the Roman law, which now began gradually to permeate the whole of Latium. Rome thus had a monopoly of business with the other cities, which were effectually isolated from each other. To us this seems a cruel and selfish policy, and so in itself it was. But we must remember that Rome had been all but destroyed off the face of the earth, and that the Latins had done nothing, so far as we know, to help her. To resist another such attack as that of the Gauls, it was absolutely necessary for Rome to control the whole military resources of Latium, and this she could not do in a loose and equal federation. She was liable not only to assaults from the Gauls, but from Etruscans, and, as we shall see directly, from Samnites, and, if we find that in the struggle for existence she was at times unjust, we may remember that there has hardly been a successful nation of which the same might not be said. She saw that Latium must become Roman if either Rome or the Latins were to survive, and she devised the principle of isolation with this object.

From this time all Latins served in Roman armies

nominally as allies, but in reality as subjects; and all Latins who became Roman citizens served in the Roman legions. When a military colony was founded, it might be either Roman or Latin; but a Latin colony meant not necessarily a collection of Latins; it might admit any one—Roman, Latin, or other—who threw in his lot with the new city and accepted the two rights of trade and marriage described above. Thus the term Latin came to mean not so much a man of a certain stock as a man with a certain legal position, and so it continued for many centuries, while the new power rising to prominence in the world came to be known not as Latin, but as Roman.

The last and decisive battle with the Latins took its name, as we saw, from Mount Vesuvius, and the reader who knows the map of Italy will ask how it came to be fought so far south of Latium, in the large and fertile plain of Campania, near the modern city of Naples. The answer is that a powerful State, such as Rome was now becoming, is liable to be appealed to by weaker communities when in trouble; and the Campanians, attacked by the hill-men from the central mountainous region of the Samnites, had appealed for help to Rome. This was given, but the Romans found it necessary to make peace with these Samnites, and left the Campanians in the lurch, and then the latter threw in their lot with the Latins, and the Latin war drifted south to Campania. At the end of that war they were treated in much the same way as the Latins; and thus Rome now found herself presiding with irresistible force over a territory that included both the plains of western Italy and all its most valuable land, and over a confederacy in which all the advantages were on her side, and all the resources of the members under her control.

But to be mistress of these two plains was not as yet to be mistress of Italy. Those plains, and especially the southern and more valuable one, had to be defended from the mountaineers of the central highlands of the peninsula: a region which the reader should at this point of our story study carefully in his map. Towards the end of the Latin war these highlanders, Samnites, as the Romans called them, had ceased raiding the Campanian plain, for they in their turn had to defend southern Italy against an unexpected enemy. The strong and wealthy Greek merchant-city of Tarentum, just inside the 'heel' of Italy, destined to play an important part in Italian history for the next century, had lately had its lands raided by the Samnites (and their kin the Lucanians to the south of them), and had called in Greeks from oversea to help them. Here we come into touch with Greek history, just at the time when Alexander the Great was the leading figure in the Greek world. A Spartan king came over to aid Tarentum, and lost his life in so doing; then Alexander of Epirus, an uncle of the great conqueror, was induced to come: but after a period of success against the Samnites, he was assassinated. It is said that Rome came to an understanding with him, and it is likely enough; there must have been men in the great Council at Rome who were already accustomed to look far ahead, and keep themselves informed of what was going on far away in Italy and even beyond the Italian seas. Her long struggle for existence had taught her venerable statesmen the arts of diplomacy, and we are not surprised to learn that after the death of Alexander she began to form alliances in that far country between the Samnites and Tarentum, much of which was rich and fertile, in order that when the inevitable struggle with the hill-men should come, she might have them enclosed between two foes—herself and Latium on the north and west, and the Apulians and Greeks in the south and east. It seemed as if her power and prestige must continually go forward, or collapse altogether; the same alternative that faced the English in India in the eighteenth century and later. In neither case did the advancing power fully realize what the future was to be.

The inevitable struggle with the Samnites came, and lasted many years. We need not pursue it in detail, and indeed the details are mostly untrustworthy as they have come down to us; but one episode in it is told so explicitly, and has become so famous, that it deserves a place in our sketch as showing that hard feeling of national self-interest, without a touch of chivalry, that is gradually emerging as the guide of Roman action in her progress towards universal dominion.

A strong Roman army, under the command of both consuls, was pushing to the south through the mountains, and fell into a trap in a defile called the Caudine Forks,[1] a name never forgotten by the Romans. All attempts to escape were vain, and they were forced to capitulate. The terms dictated by Pontius the Samnite general were these: the consuls were to bind themselves on behalf of the Senate to agree to evacuate Samnium and Campania and the fortresses (*coloniae*) which had been planted there, and to make peace with the Samnites as with an equal power. The consuls bound themselves by a solemn rite, and the army was allowed to go home, after being sent under the yoke, i.e. under a kind of archway consisting of one spear resting on two upright ones: this was an old Italian

---

[1] The Latin word is *fauces*, i.e. jaws, etymologically the same word as the *hause* of our Lakeland, which means a narrow pass.

custom of dealing with a conquered army, which may have originally had a religious signification. When the disgraced legions reached Rome, and the consuls summoned the Senate to ratify their bond with Pontius, the Fathers, as they were called, positively refused to do so. The consuls and all who had made themselves responsible for the terms were sent back to Pontius as his prisoners, *but not the army*. His indignation was great, for he knew that Samnium had lost her chance, and would never have it again. The consuls, of course, had no power to bind the Senate, and the Samnite terms were such as the Senate could not accept as the result of a single disaster caused by a general's blunder: that was not the way in which the Romans carried on war. But the disgraced army should have been sent back too, and the Senate and people knew it. The speech which the later Roman historian puts into the mouth of Pontius to express his indignation shows that some feeling of shame at this dishonourable action had come down in the minds of many generations.

The last effort of this long struggle against Rome was a desperate attempt to combine the forces of Samnites, Etruscans and Gauls: the idea was to separate her armies and thus crush her in detail. Even this was a failure, and without going into the doubtful stories of the fighting, we may ask why it was so. Beyond all doubt the Roman power was for a time in very great peril; but in the end it prevailed, and this is a good moment for pausing to think about the advantages that Rome's genius for organization had secured for herself; advantages which no other Italian stock seemed able to acquire.

First, she had learnt how to use with profit her geographical position; to north, south and east she could send armies to strike in different directions at the same time; and she must have devised some means (though we do not know the method) of keeping up communication between these armies. The stories seem to suggest that the commanders of this period belonged to a very few noble families whose members had spent their whole lives in fighting—not indeed merely in fighting battles, but in carrying on war: the Fabii and Papirii are particularly prominent. These veterans must have come to know the art of war thoroughly, as it could then be applied in Italy, and also the details of the country in which they had to fight.

Secondly, the efforts of these tough old heroes were admirably seconded by the home government, i.e. the Senate, because this assembly consisted of men of the like military experience, and the leaders among them were themselves generals, men who had been consuls and had led armies. Though at this very time, as we shall see, there was a strong tendency towards popular government, yet in the direction of war we find no sign that the monopoly of the old families was questioned; and as their interests and their experience were all of the same type, they could act together with a unanimity which was probably unknown to their enemies. The fact that Rome always at this time, and indeed at all times, negotiated and kept in touch with the *aristocracies* in the Italian cities, shows how completely the noble families had gained control over the management of diplomacy as well as war.

Thirdly, Rome was now beginning to learn the art of securing the conquered country by means of military roads and fortresses (*coloniae*): an art to which she held firmly throughout her history, and to which the geography even of Roman Britain bears ample testimony. My readers will do well to fix their attention for a moment on three of these colonies which were founded during this long war; they are by no means the only ones, but they serve well to show the extent of the Roman power in Italy at this time, as well as the means taken to secure it. The first is Narnia (founded 299 B.C.) far up the Tiber valley on a military road afterwards known as the Flaminian Way: this was an outpost, with quick communication with Rome, against both Etruscans and Gauls. The second, Fregellae, a city with a sad future, was some seventy miles to the south-east of Rome, on a road called the Latin Way, but beyond the limits of Latium proper, commanding, in fact, the passes between Latium and Campania; it was in a beautiful situation near the junction of two rivers, and became in time a most prosperous city. For the third colony we must look much farther south on the map, at the south-eastern end of the mass of the Samnite highlands: this was Venusia, with 20,000 colonists, destined to separate the Samnites from the Greeks and other inhabitants of the heel and toe of Italy. It stood on the most famous of all the great roads, the Via Appia, which after leaving Rome ran nearer the coast than the Latin Way, but joined it in Campania, and then ran across the hilly country to Venusia, and eventually to Brundisium (Brindisi), which also became a colony fifty years later.

These three advantages, duly considered, will help the reader to understand to some extent how the prize of Italian presidency fell to Rome and not to another city: and they will also explain why Rome emerged safe and stronger than ever from another peril that was now to threaten her existence.

The great colony of Venusia, as we saw, was meant to separate the Greeks of southern Italy from the

highlanders of Samnium. Of the Greek cities by far
the most powerful was Tarentum, then ruled by a
selfish and ill-conditioned democracy, apt to be
continually worrying its neighbours. That Rome
should sooner or later come into collision with Tarentum was inevitable; but the Senate tried to avoid this,
knowing that the Tarentines would appeal to some
Greek power beyond sea to help them. Now just
across the Adriatic, in Epirus, there was a king of
Greek descent who was looking out for a chance of
glory by imitating Alexander the Great; for Alexander's
marvellous career had stirred up a restless spirit of
adventure in the free-lances of the generation that
succeeded him. Pyrrhus seems to have fancied that
he could act the part of a knight-errant in freeing the
Greeks of the west from the barbarians—from the
Romans that is, and the Carthaginians, who were at
the moment in alliance. When the inevitable quarrel
with Rome came, and Tarentum invited him, he
crossed the sea with a small but capable force, determined to put an end to this new power that was
threatening to swallow up the Greek cities. But he
had to learn, and through him the Greek world had to
learn as a whole, that the new power was made of
sterner stuff than any that had yet arisen in the
Mediterranean basin.

Pyrrhus began with a victory, not far from Tarentum;
it was won chiefly by some elephants which he had
brought with him to frighten the Roman cavalry.
This shook the loyalty of many Italian communities,
but the Senate was unmoved. The ablest diplomatist
in Pyrrhus's service made no impression on that body
of resolute men, trained by long experience to look on
a single defeat as only a 'regrettable incident' in a
long war. "Rome never negotiates while foreign troops

are on Italian soil'; so, according to the story, the aged Appius Claudius told the Greek envoy in the Senate-house. Then Pyrrhus tried a march on Rome; but he had to learn, like another invader after him, that the nearer he drew to the city the more difficult his task became. A second victory was far less decisive and almost fruitless, and Pyrrhus most unwisely evacuated Italy. The king crossed to Sicily to deliver the Sicilian Greeks from Carthage, and this he did brilliantly, but the fickle Greeks soon grew tired of him. Returning to Italy, he fought one more battle with the Romans, at Beneventum in Samnium, and lost it. Foiled everywhere, he left Italy, with Rome more firmly established than ever in the supremacy of the whole peninsula: for Tarentum, with its fine harbour, its almost impregnable citadel, and its fleet, fell soon afterwards into the hands of the Romans.

Almost the whole Italian peninsula was now Roman; or perhaps it is truer to say that Rome had become an Italian state. It was a wonderful work: perhaps the most wonderful that Rome ever achieved. The military part of it was the result mainly of *constantia*, steady perseverance and refusal to accept defeat; the political organization was the result of good sense and good temper combined with an inflexible will, and a shrewd perception of the real and permanent interests of Rome. In the third century B.C., at which we have now arrived, Italy may be described as a kind of federation, in which each city has its own alliance with the leading one, and no alliance with any other. Each has its own government and administers its own law, but places all its military resources at the disposal of the Roman government. The fighting power of the future was to be Italy under Roman leadership, and all questions of foreign policy were decided by Rome alone. There was no general council of the whole confederacy. The Roman Senate controlled an ever-increasing mass of detailed and varied business, having to deal with Latins, Italians of the old stocks, Etruscans, Greeks and Gauls. How the business was done we cannot tell: not a single contemporary record of it is left. One glimpse of that wonderful Senate at work would be worth all descriptions of the battles of that century.

Before the close of the third century B.C. that Senate, instead of directing a further steady advance, had been forced to defend the State against an invader, in the most terrible life-and-death struggle ever experienced by any people. But in the next chapter I must pause to try and explain wherein consisted the nerve-power, the mental and material fibre, of the people destined to rule the world.

CHAPTER III

THE TRAINING OF THE ROMAN CHARACTER

I HAVE mentioned some outward circumstances which gave Rome an early training in war and diplomacy, and in particular her geographical position, exposing her to constant attack, and yet giving her good chance of striking back and advancing. But to accomplish all that was told of her in the last chapter, more than this was surely needed. There must have been a quality in this people, individually and as a whole, fitting them to withstand so much storm and stress, and to emerge from disaster with renewed strength to take in hand the work of conquest and government. We need not, indeed, assume that the people of this one city were naturally of stronger character than others, than their kinsfolk of the Latin cities or other Italians of the same great race. All these immigrating stocks, which spread themselves, long before history begins, over a primitive population of which we know little or nothing, were probably much the same in physical and mental build; a fact which will help us to understand how they all came eventually to be able to unite together as the centre of a great empire. But the quality or character, which I am to try and explain in this chapter, was more strongly stamped upon the citizens of Rome than on those of other cities, owing to the more continual call for them in her case; for all our qualities and habits can be made more sure and lasting by constant exercise.

Discipline and duty are the two words which best explain, if they do not exactly express, the quality here meant; the habit of obedience to authority, which is the necessary condition of the power of governing, and that sense of duty which lies at the root of the habit and the power. This aptitude for discipline and this sense of duty can be traced both in the private and the public life of early Rome, in the life of the family and in the life of the State. Let us be clear at once that the individual as such was not as yet an important item of society; society was based on a system of groups, and the individual played no part in it in these early times except as the member of a group, either a group of kin (*gens*), or a local and administrative group (*pagus, curia*). But the only group with which we are concerned in this little book, the smallest of all, was the *familia*, another of those immortal words which we have inherited from the Latin language. This shall be explained first, in order to find the discipline and duty of that family life: then we will take the State, and follow out the same habits reproducing themselves in a more complicated social and political union.

This word *familia* did not mean exactly what we mean by family; household would perhaps come nearer to it, if we understand by household a group of individuals supporting itself on the land. It meant not only father, mother, and children, but also their dependants, whether bond or free. These, if bond, were slaves (*servi*), prisoners of war and the children of such prisoners, or persons who had forfeited their liberty through debt: if free, they were clients, who for some reason had become attached to the *familia* in an inferior position, and looked to it for subsistence and protection. And our picture is not complete unless we take into account also the divine members of the group, dwelling in the house or on the land, to whom the human members looked for protection and prosperity in all the walks of life. Chief among these were : the spirit of the hearth-fire, Vesta; the Penates, spirits of the store-closet and its contents; the Lar, the guardian spirit of the cultivated land, or, as some think, of a departed ancestor; and the Genius of the head of the family, which enabled him to beget children and so continue the collective life of the group. Though these spirits—they are hardly yet deities—naturally seem to us mere fancies of the primitive Roman mind, they were to that mind itself as real and active as any human member of the group, and we must try to think of them as such, for they played a very important part in the development of the quality we wish to realize.

Now this group, or rather the human part of it, lived under a very simple and effective form of government. It was under the absolute control of a head, the father and husband; or, if more than one family lived together, the oldest living father and husband. Over wife and children he had a father's power (*patria potestas*), and they were said to be in his *hand*; over the slaves he had a master's power (*dominium*): to his clients he was *patronus*, or quasi-father. His power over wife and children was absolute, but it was kept from being arbitrary by a wholesome custom, of immense importance in all its results throughout Roman history, of seeking the advice of a council of relations before taking any extreme step in the way of punishment for serious offences. This was an obligation, a duty, on his part, enforced by no law, but by what may be well called an even more powerful sovereign than law— the custom of the ancestors (*mos majorum*). His power over his client, or his freed slave if he had any such, was restrained by customs of mutual obligation, which eventually found their way into law. His power over his slaves was, however, not only absolute but arbitrary, and so continued down to the latest period of Roman history; yet the slave, we must not forget, was really a member of the *familia*, and as such was probably treated as a human being, necessary to the life of the group, and even partaking to some extent in its religious worship.

Let us see how this system of government would work out in the practical life of a *familia* settled on the land, as all such groups were during at least a great part of the period we have been tracing: for the city itself was mainly used as a fortress, into which the farming families would come in time of peril, and in which they would in course of time possess a town dwelling as well as a farm, like the leading families of our English shires in the Middle Ages. The *pater-familias* directed all the operations of the farm, no one disputing his authority: and he decided all quarrels among his subjects and punished all offences. The necessary work of the house, the cooking, and the spinning of wool for the garments of the members (which were then entirely woollen), he left to his wife and daughters: and thus the wife came to exercise a kind of authority of her own, which raised her far above the position of a 'squaw', and gave her in course of time a great influence, though an indirect one, in social life. Not only had all the members their work to do, under this strict control, in keeping themselves alive and clothed, but they all had their duties to the divine members, on whom they believed themselves dependent for their health and wealth. There were simple acts of worship every day and at every meal, in which the children joined; we may almost think of the Head as a priest and of the children as his acolytes. And at certain days, fixed in ancient times by a council of Heads, and later in the city by a calendar, the families of a district (*pagus*) would join together in religious festivities, after harvest, for example, or after the autumn sowing, to honour and propitiate the spirit of the harvested grain or of the sown seed. These were often accompanied by games and races, and so the life was saved from becoming too sombre and monotonous. But though discipline was not allowed to destroy freedom and enjoyment, the life was on the whole a routine of command and obedience, of discipline and duty.

What of the education which should perpetuate these habits? Unluckily we have no contemporary record of it for these early times, and must guess at it chiefly from what we know of the bringing up of his son by the elder Cato, a strenuous believer in the old methods, in the second century B.C. As we might expect, it seems to have been an education in the active practical life of the farm, and in reverence, obedience, and modesty of demeanour. Cato taught his boy not only to work, to ride, to box, and to swim, but to shun all indecency; and was himself 'as careful not to utter an indecent word before his son, as he would have been in the presence of the Vestal Virgins'. He wrote histories for his son in large letters, so that he might learn something of the illustrious deeds of the ancient Romans, and of their customs. In his time an education of the mind was beginning to come into vogue, as well as one of the will; but in the period we have been surveying this must have been of the most meagre kind. Yet it is possible that the idea of active duty to the State and its deities, as well as to the family and its presiding spirits, was all the more vividly kept up in the absence of intellectual interests. As life in the city became more usual, the boys of good families had more opportunity of learning what was meant by duty to the State; they accompanied their fathers to hear funeral orations on eminent citizens, and were even admitted to meetings of the Senate. In this way they must have developed a shrewdness and practical sagacity invaluable to them in after life.

There is a story, preserved by the elder Cato, which so well illustrates this and other features of that early Roman life, that I shall insert it here, whether or no it be strictly true. A boy who had been with his father to the Senate was asked by an inquisitive mother what the Fathers of the Senate had been discussing. The boy answered that he was strictly forbidden to tell, which only excited his mother's curiosity the more, and made her press him hard. At last he invented what Cato calls a shrewd and witty falsehood: he said that the Senate had been discussing whether it were better for the State that one man should have two wives or one wife two husbands. Much alarmed, she went and told other matrons, and next day they crowded weeping to the Senate House, to petition that one wife might have two husbands rather than one husband two wives. The astonishment of the senators was dispelled by the boy, who stood out in the midst and told his tale; and from that time no boy was allowed to be present at debate save this one, who was thus rewarded for his honesty and shrewdness.

This good old Roman story may aptly bring us to the second part of my subject in this chapter, the training of the citizen in the service of the State. But let us pause here for a moment to consider what was the Roman idea of the State and its function.

In Italy, as in Greece, the State took the form of a city, with more or less of territory on which to subsist; in the heart of the city was the life of the State. And it is true of Italy as of Greece that the process of rising to the city from the life of farm or village was one of immense importance for humanity, enabling man to advance from the idea of a bare material subsistence to that of moral and intellectual progress. This is the advance to what Aristotle called 'good life' as distinguished from life simply. He meant that in the lower stage man has not time or stimulus to develop art, literature, law, philosophy: all his strength is spent in struggle and endeavour—struggle partly with Nature, partly with human enemies whom he is ill able to resist. The city-state supplied him not only with opportunity for a higher life, but with nutriment to maintain it.

But the Italians never drew from this new form of social life the same amount, the same quality of nutriment, as did the Greeks. Rome did indeed draw enough to fertilize the germs of much that was most valuable in her own character, and to educate herself for the practical work she was to do in the world. But the last chapter will have shown that, unlike most Greek city-states, she was forced by circumstances to continue for centuries a life of struggle and endeavour. She had constant difficulty in keeping herself alive and free, and, as we shall see, she was hardly ever without internal as well as external perils. In Greece many States found leisure to rest and enjoy the exercise of their higher instincts—enjoyment which led to the production of works of art and literature: leisure, too, to reflect and inquire about Nature in man and outside him, and so to develop philosophy and science for the eternal benefit of mankind. But all the strength of Rome was used in the struggle for existence, which gradually led her on to conquest and dominion. As we left her at the end of the last chapter, the leading city of Italy, she might indeed have passed from struggle to leisure, and so to thought and inquiry, turning to account the gifts of the various peoples of Italy, Etruscans, Gauls, Greeks, as well as her own kin. But the long and terrible struggle with Carthage, to be told in the next chapter, effectually destroyed this chance. Her strength was spent when it was over, and when her chance came to sit down (so to speak), and think, she could not do it. Still, her long training in practical endeavour had its due result; and the ideas of duty and discipline, of law and order, which had carried her through so many perils, never wholly vanished from the Roman mind. Let us turn to trace the progress of those ideas in the life of the city-state of Rome.

When we first begin to see clearly into the working of the Roman State, what chiefly strikes us is the unlimited power of the magistrate in all the departments of government. Just as the head of the family had an absolute power over its members, so had the king (*rex*) an unlimited power over the citizens. In the family the word for this power was *potestas*, but in the State it was called *imperium*—one of the greatest words ever coined, surviving to the present day in many familiar forms. For the Roman it expressed more strikingly than any other the idea of discipline in the State: it stamped on his mind the inherited conviction that *lawful authority* must be implicitly obeyed. Not unlawful authority, ill gotten by fraud or violence; for such power the word *imperium* could never be used: but authority entrusted to an individual by the human members of the State, and sanctioned by the consent of its divine members. For the *imperium* must be conferred upon its holder by an act of the people, and the gods must give their consent by favourable omens; both processes, the passing of the law, and the obtaining of the *auspicia*, must be gone through according to certain traditional methods, and the slightest flaw in these would make the choice of the magistrate invalid. But once legally in his hands, the *imperium* was irresistible; its outward symbols, the rods and axes of the lictors, accompanied its holder wherever he went, to remind the Roman that the first duty of a citizen was obedience to constituted authority.

This word *imperium* stood for three different kinds of power. First, the king was supreme in matters of religion, for he was responsible for the good relations between the human and divine inhabitants of the city, for 'the peace of the gods' as it was called. If this peace, or covenant, were not kept up, it was believed that the State could not prosper—the very life of the State depended on it.

But now let us note a point of the utmost importance in the development of Roman public life. The king could not perform this duty entirely by himself; no single man could have the necessary knowledge of all the details of ancient religious custom. So he was assisted by a small board of skilled experts called *pontifices*, perhaps also by another board of *augurs*, skilled in the methods of discovering the divine will by omens. Thus the *imperium* in religious matters, though still legally unlimited, was saved from becoming arbitrary and violating ancestral custom: the king is entrusted with power which he uses in accordance with the advice of sages.

Secondly, *imperium* stood for the supreme judicial power, for the maintenance of peace between individual citizens. The king had an unlimited power not only in deciding disputes but in inflicting punishments, even that of death. But here again, though his power was absolute, it was not arbitrary. Custom governed the State even more than he did, and his work was to see that custom was obeyed. In order to make sure that this duty was rightly performed, he was provided with a council of elderly men (*senatores*), fathers of families, whose advice custom compelled him to ask, though it did not compel him to take it. Here, then, the exercise of discipline was combined with a sense of duty and obligation, as in the life of the family; the Senate of the State was the same in principle as the council of relations in the family.

Thirdly, *imperium* stood for the absolute power of the commander in war: and here, as we might expect, custom seems hardly to have interfered with it. A Roman king in war was outside the custom of his own State, beyond the reach of the protection of his own deities, and under the influence of unknown ones. Both before starting on a campaign, and before entering the city on its return, the army had to undergo certain religious rites, which show how nervous even Romans were about leaving their own land and gods. Custom could not rule here, and the power of the general in the field remained throughout Roman history not only absolute but arbitrary. Doubtless he could, and often did, not only ask advice but take it, but he was never even morally obliged to do so: in this one department of State activity the wise judgement of the Romans left the *imperium* practically unhampered.

Such, then, was the *imperium* in the hands of the chief magistrate, the foundation-stone of the Roman government in all periods. But what of the people who obeyed it? Of the people we unluckily know hardly anything until nearly the end of the monarchical period. We do, indeed, know that, as in many Greek city-states, there was a privileged and an unprivileged class, and of these two classes a word shall be said directly. What needs here to be made clear is how this population was placed as regards duty and discipline, and our first real knowledge of this dates traditionally from the reign of the last king but one. Here we find the whole free population, privileged and unprivileged, serving in the army as a civic duty, and paying such taxes as were necessary mainly for military purposes. They served without pay, and the infantry—that is, by far the greater part—provided their own arms and equipment; the cavalry were provided with horses by the State, for horses were expensive. Those who had most property were considered as having the largest stake in the State, and therefore as bound to bear the heaviest burden. This may be seen in the order of the army for battle, for those who could afford the best equipment fought in front, the poorest and worst armed in the rear. This was the wholesome principle that governed the Roman army during the period of advance and conquest in Italy. It was an army of citizens (*populus*), all of whom served as a matter of duty, and paid taxes as a matter of duty according to their means, leaving all command to the holder of *imperium*, and the officers whom he appointed to carry out his orders.

Thus when the kingship was overthrown—and legend told how the Etruscan king, Tarquin the Proud, was so tyrannical that all classes united to drive him out—the people were thoroughly well trained in the ideas of duty and discipline, and the practical results of such a training were obedience as a habit, respect for authority and knowledge, steadiness and coolness in danger. This people did not give way to excitement, either in civil or military crises. They not only obeyed their rulers, but trusted them. They were not much given to talking, but contented themselves with action: and as talk is a more effective stimulus to quarrelling than action, they did not as yet quarrel. Though Rome was destined to pass through many political as well as military dangers in the generations to come, it was nearly four centuries before blood was shed in civil strife in her streets.

I must close this chapter with a very brief sketch of the political history of the period of advance in Italy, in order to show how their training in duty and discipline kept the people steady and sound at home.

After the expulsion of the last king the Roman State became a *respublica*—that is, literally translated, a public thing—or as we may perhaps call it, a free State. This is another of the immortal words bequeathed to modern European language by Latin speech, and its meaning is still the same for us as it was for the Romans. When Cicero, almost at the end of the life of the Roman free State, wrote to a friend, 'We have completely lost the *respublica*', he meant that it had passed from public management into the hands of private and irresponsible individuals. What were the essential marks of this 'public thing', or free State? As we might expect, they are to be found in the treatment of the *imperium*, the governmental centre of gravity, by the founders of the *respublica*.

1. To abolish the *imperium* was out of the question; no Roman ever dreamed of such a thing, for it would be like digging up the foundations of a building already in part constructed. But the *imperium* was no longer to be held for life, nor to be held by a single person. It was now to be entrusted to two magistrates instead of one, and for a year only; at the end of the year the holders, henceforward to be called Consuls or Praetors, were to lay down their insignia and resign their power, becoming simply private citizens again. Meanwhile new consuls had been elected; and the voice of the

whole people was to be heard in the election, for it was to be effected by the army of citizens, arranged according to property as in military service. Every Roman who was to obey the *imperium* was to have a voice in the election of its holders, but those who had most stake in the State, and served in the front ranks in war, were to have a preponderating voice.

2. The dread *imperium* was now not only limited in the period of its tenure, but the possibility of an arbitrary use of it was averted in two ways. First, the two consuls had a veto on each other's action, and both at home and in the field they took it in turn to exercise the *imperium*. Secondly, they could not put a citizen to death in the city unless the people in their assembly sanctioned it; in the field the Romans wisely left the *imperium* unlimited, feeling, as we still feel, that military discipline needs a more forceful sanction than civil. And besides these two restrictions, the council of elders, the Senate, was retained to act as a general advising body for the consuls, who, however, themselves had the power of filling up vacancies in it from time to time. We do not know exactly what its composition was at this time; but it is certain that all who had held the *imperium* had seats in it, as men whose service and experience best entitled them to advise and criticize their successors. This principle, that ex-magistrates should be members of the Senate, was adhered to at all times, and eventually made this great council into the most effective assembly of men of capacity and experience in practical life that the world has ever seen.

Before we leave the *imperium*, for the present, one interesting fact must be noted. The Romans were not afraid to withdraw for a time these restrictions on the magistrate's power, and to revert to absolute government, if they thought it necessary for the safety of the State. In moments of great peril, civil or military, the consul, on the advice of the Senate, would appoint a single individual to hold office for a fixed time with unlimited *imperium*; and in this case the assembly was not called on even to ratify the choice, so great was the trust reposed in the fathers of the State. They did not call this single magistrate by the hated name of Rex, but used another word well known in Latium, Dictator. The institution was of the utmost value to a people constantly in a state of struggle and endeavour, and shows well the practical sagacity which a long training in duty and discipline had already developed.

But this practical sagacity was to be put to many a hard test in the period we sketched in the last chapter. No sooner was the *respublica* established, than a great question pressed for solution, that of the mutual relations of the privileged and unprivileged classes. What was really the origin of this distinction of class we do not yet know, and perhaps never shall. Here the fact must suffice that the privileged, the patricians as they were called, the representatives of families belonging to the old clans (*gentes*), were alone deemed capable of preserving the peace between citizens and gods, or between the citizens themselves, and therefore they alone could hold the *imperium* and take the auspices. Both classes served in the army and voted at elections, but without the chance of holding the *imperium* the plebeians were helpless. Yet it is quite certain that they had grievances of their own, and real ones. We must think of them as in the main small holders of land, with little or no capital, and constantly obliged to borrow either in the form of money or stock. They became debtors to the rich, who would usually be the patricians, and the old customary law of debt was hard and even savage.

The result of this was, according to the traditional story, that once at least, if not twice, they actually *struck*; they left their work and went off in a body, threatening to found a new city some miles farther up the Tiber. They knew well that they were indispensable to the State as soldiers, and the patricians knew it too. Fortunately, the plebeians also knew that the State, with all its traditions of religion and government, of duty and discipline, was indispensable to themselves. They knew nothing of the forms and formulae which were deemed necessary for the maintenance of peace with gods and men. They could not carry away with them the gods of the city, under whose protection they and their forefathers had lived. They would simply be adrift, without oars or rudder, and such a position was absolutely unthinkable. So they returned to the city—so the story runs—and the result was a compromise, the first of a long series of compromises which finally made Rome into a compact and united commonwealth, and enabled her to tide over three centuries of continual struggle and endeavour. The story of these compromises is too long and complicated to be told in this book, but the successive stages can briefly be pointed out.

Soon after the strike, or secession, the plebeians were authorized to elect magistrates, or more strictly officers, of their own, to protect them from any arbitrary use of the *imperium*; these were called Tribunes, because the assembly that chose them was arranged according to tribes, local divisions in which both patricians and plebeians were registered for taxpaying purposes. The good will of the patricians in making this concession is seen in the fact that the tribunes of the plebs (as they were henceforward called) were placed under the protection of the gods (*sacrosancti*), so that any one violating them was made liable to divine anger. As the plebeians grew more numerous and indispensable, their assembly and officers became steadily more powerful, and eventually won the right to pass laws binding the whole State.

Again, it was not long before their ignorance of the customary law and its methods of procedure found a remedy. A code of law was drawn up in twelve tables, containing partly old custom now for the first time written down, partly new rules, some of them perhaps imported from Athens. Of this code we still possess many fragments, which show plainly that it was meant for all citizens, whatever their social standing. 'The idea of legislating for a class . . . is strikingly absent. The code is thoroughly Roman in its caution and good sense, its respect for the past, which it disregards only when old customs violate the rules of common sense, and its judicious contempt for symmetry.' [1] As the historian Tacitus said of it long afterwards, it was 'the consummation of equal right'. And it was the source of the whole mighty river of Roman law, ever increasing in volume, which still serves to irrigate the field of modern European civilization.

There was to be a long and bitter contest before the plebeians forced their way into the central patrician stronghold of the *imperium*, but even this was accomplished without civil war or bloodshed. We hear of a series of evasive manoeuvres by the patricians, who naturally believed that all would go wrong if the duty of keeping 'the peace of the gods' were committed to men whom the gods could not be supposed to take count of. But these patrician consuls and senators

[1] Greenidge, *Roman Public Life*, p. 105.

were responsible for the State's existence, and it could not exist without the plebeians; the two classes were authorized by law to intermarry, which (strange to say) had been unlawful hitherto, and then the old class-feeling and prejudice, far exceeding in force any such feeling known to us now, gradually subsided. By the middle of the fourth century B.C., not only could a plebeian be consul, but one of the two consuls *must* be a plebeian. And before that century was over the old patrician nobility was beginning to disappear, giving way to a new one based on the leading idea of *good service done for the State*. If a man had held the consulship, no matter whether he were patrician or plebeian, he became *nobilis*—i.e. distinguished—and so, too, did his family. The great Roman aristocracy of later times consisted of the descendants of men who had thus become distinguished.

I will conclude this chapter with a few words about one remarkable institution which well illustrates the Roman instinct for duty and discipline. It was in this period, 443 B.C., according to the traditional date, that a new magistracy was established, intended at first merely to relieve the consuls of difficult duties for which in that warlike age they had no sufficient leisure, but destined eventually to become even a higher object of ambition than the consulship itself. The Roman love of order made it necessary to be sure that every citizen was justly and legally a citizen, that he fulfilled his duties in the army, and paid his taxes according to a right estimate of his property. Every four or five years an inquiry had to be made with this object in view, and two Censors, holding office for a year and a half, were now elected to undertake it. These Censors, though they had no *imperium*, were autocratic; their decisions were final, and they could not be called to account

for any official act. They were almost always—
in later times invariably—reverend seniors who had
held the consulship, men in whose justice and wisdom
the people could put implicit confidence. And such
confidence was needed; for their power of examination
easily became extended from details of registration to
the personal conduct of the citizen in almost every
sphere of life. All heads of families might be questioned about their performance of family duties, and
any shameful cruelty to a slave, or injustice to a client,
or neglect of children, might be punished by removal
from the list of tribesmen; and this meant *infamia*
(civic disgrace), a terrible word, greatly dreaded by the
Roman. Neglect of land or other property, useless
luxury, bad faith in contracts or legal guardianship—
all came in course of time to be taken count of by the
censors. A senator might have his name struck off
the list of the Senate, and a cavalry soldier might be
removed from the roll, if the horse provided him by
the State were ill cared for, or if in any other way he
were deemed unworthy of his position.

It may be hard for us to understand how such a
power of inquisition can have been submitted to in a
free State. But apart from the age and standing of
the holders of this office, and the Roman habit of
obedience to constituted authority, there are two facts
that will help us to understand it. One is simple: the
censors were *collegae* like the consuls; each had a veto
on the action of the other, and if that veto were not
used, if they were unanimous in condemning a citizen,
the authority of their decision was naturally irresistible.
The other fact is harder for a modern to understand.
There was a religious element in the work of the
censors; the final act of a censorship was the religious
'purification' (*lustratio*) of the whole citizen body,

with sacrifice and prayer, in the field of Mars outside the walls of the city. What exactly a Roman of that day believed, or rather felt, to be the result of this rite, we can only guess; but we can be sure that he was convinced that the life of the State would be imperilled without it, and that this conviction was strong enough to compel him to submit to the whole process of which it was the consummation.

CHAPTER IV

THE STRUGGLE WITH CARTHAGE
AND HANNIBAL

In these days sober students of history wisely leave the oft-told stories of war and battle, and busy themselves rather with questions of social life, public and private economy, and the history of religion, morals and scientific inquiry. But there are a few wars, great struggles of nation against nation, which will always have an absorbing interest: partly because of their dramatic character, partly because of their far-reaching consequences; and the long fight between Rome and Carthage is assuredly one of these. On the Carthaginian side it produced two of the most extraordinary men, father and son, of whom history has anywhere to tell; and on the Roman side it gives us a vivid picture of the most marvellous endurance during long years of extreme peril that we can find in the annals of any people. And probably no war was ever so pregnant of results for good and ill alike. It welded the whole of Italy south of the Alps into a united country under the rule of Rome, and launched the Romans on a new career of conquest beyond the sea; it laid the foundations of the Roman Empire as we now think of that great system. Yet it left Italy in a state of economic distress from which it is hardly untrue to say that she has never fully recovered, and it changed the character of the Roman people, rich and poor alike, for the worse rather than the better.

In order to see clearly how it came about, we must once more look at the map of Italy; a map of modern Italy will do well enough. Let the reader remember that as yet Rome had control only over the central and southern parts of the whole of what is now the republic of Italy, and that two other parts of that republic, which every Italian now regards as essential to its unity, were in other hands. There were: first, the great alluvial plain of the river Po (Padus); secondly, the island of Sicily: strategically speaking, these lie on the two flanks of the Roman dominion, to north and south respectively. Any power holding central Italy, to be safe from invasion, must be in possession of these two positions, as a long series of wars has clearly shown, beginning with the two now to be sketched. The magnificent plain of the Po, stretching from the great Alpine barrier to the Apennines which look down on the Gulf of Genoa, the richest land in all Italy, was then in the hands of warlike Gallic tribes, who had settled there before the time when they struck southward and captured Rome itself; these might again become a serious danger, as indeed they proved to be in this very war. The island of Sicily was, and had long been, a bone of contention between the Greek settlers who had long ago built cities on the most favourable points of its coast, and the traders of the Phoenician city of Carthage just opposite to it on the coast of Africa. Sicily was rich in harbours, and like the plain of the Po, also rich in corn, olive, and vine; and the Greeks had held on to it so persistently that with the recent help of Pyrrhus they had for a moment been in almost complete possession of the island. But they foolishly deserted Pyrrhus at the critical moment, and now again the Carthaginians had recovered it, all but the kingdom of Hiero of Syracuse, stretching along the eastern coast under Mount Etna. Carthaginian fleets cruised round the island, and were often seen off the coasts of Italy as well. For Carthage was the mistress of the seas in all the western part of the Mediterranean basin.

Carthage was a daughter of the Canaanite city of Tyre, belonging to that seafaring people known in history as Phoenicians, whom the Israelites had pushed down to the coast of Palestine without subduing them. The genius of the Phoenicians was for trade, and the splendid position of Carthage, near the modern Tunis, with a rich corn-growing country in the rear, had helped her merchant princes to establish by degrees what may loosely be called an empire of trading settlements extending not only along the African coast, but over that of Sardinia and southern and eastern Spain, and including Sicily, as we have seen. To maintain this empire she had to keep up great fleets, and huge docks in her own port; but as her Phoenician population was largely occupied with trade, she had to rely for her crews and also for her land forces largely on the native Africans whom she had subdued, or on mercenaries hired from other races with whom she came in contact. Though this was a weak point in her armour, she was far the greatest power in the western seas, and any other people ambitious of power in that region would have to reckon with her. So far she had been on friendly terms with Rome, and we still have the text of three treaties between the two states; but the latest of these shows signs of mutual distrust, and Rome had now risen so high that a collision was all but inevitable. A people ruling in Italy cannot afford to have a rival in Sicily and also in undisputed command of the sea.

The collision came in the year 264 B.C., and it was the immediate result of an act of bad judgement and also of bad faith on the part of the Romans. There would be no need to mention this here if it did not illustrate a trait in the Roman character which is becoming more marked as Rome is drawn more and more into diplomatic relations with other states. The habit of order and discipline at home did not bring with it a sense of justice and honour in dealing with foreigners. The Roman practical view of life, which did not include education of the mind and feeling, was not favourable to the growth of generous conduct except towards a fellow-citizen. The Latin word *virtus*, which expresses the practical duties of a citizen, does not suggest honourable dealing outside the civic boundary. Some mental imagination was needed for higher aims to make themselves felt in public life; 'slimness', as the Boers of the Transvaal used to call it, is too often characteristic of Roman diplomacy; and hardness, not always stopping short of cruelty, is henceforward constantly to be found in their conduct towards a beaten foe.

A rascally band of mercenaries, Italians by birth, who had been in the Syracusan service, had seized on the old Greek city of Messana—the modern Messina. The city lay on the Sicilian side of the strait which still bears its name, and looked at from an Italian point of view might be called the key to Sicily. Exactly opposite to it was Rhegium (Reggio), another Greek city which had been treated in the same way by another band of brigands; but these had been at once cleared out by orders from Rome. At Messana the task naturally devolved on Hiero, the king of Syracuse, a young man of ability who had lately made a treaty with Rome; but when he made the attempt, the brigands appealed for help both to Rome and to Carthage. The plain duty of the Senate was to support their ally Hiero, or to leave the applicants to their fate. But the Carthaginians might then establish themselves at Messana, and that must have seemed to a Roman a thing not to be permitted. The Senate hesitated for once, and finally referred the matter to the people, who voted to support the mercenaries against an ally of the Roman State. This act of bad faith and bad policy cost the Romans a valuable ally, and a war with Carthage that lasted without a break for twenty-three years.

It would be waste of space in this little book to go into the details of this long and wearisome war, which can be read in any history of Rome. It was, of course, in the main a naval war, and the Romans had as yet no fleet to speak of. But now was seen the advantage of a united Italy. The difficulty was overcome by enlisting the services of Greek and Etruscan sailors and ship-builders; a Carthaginian war-vessel, wrecked on the Italian coast, served as a model, and a large fleet was soon ready for sea, with which, strange to say, the Roman commanders succeeded in the course of a few years in clearing the Italian and Sicilian seas of the enemy, and even contrived to transport an army of invasion to Carthaginian territory. This astonishing feat was accomplished simply by the invention of a device for grappling with the enemy's ships, so that they could be boarded by Roman soldiers acting as 'marines'. And during this first half of the war they also renewed their alliance with Hiero, and conquered the whole of Sicily, with the exception of the strong city of Lilybaeum (now Marsala).

But all these good results were thrown away by the folly of the Roman Senate. Now that they had crossed the sea and entered on a new sphere of action, they seemed for the moment to have lost the prudence and wisdom that had won them the headship of Italy. They had two consular armies in Africa which seemed to have Carthage herself in their grip; but when she sued for peace they offered her impossible terms, and about the same time actually recalled one of the two consuls with his army to Italy. The old Phoenician spirit revived, and turned to desperate courage: an able Greek soldier of fortune, Xanthippus, took the Carthaginian army in hand, and before long the remaining Roman army was utterly destroyed, and its commander Regulus was a prisoner. This is the Regulus of one of the most famous of Roman stories, and one of the most beautiful of Horace's *Odes*. He is said to have gone to Rome on *parole* with an embassy, and on its failure to have returned a captive to Carthage, where he was put to a cruel death. Many critics now reject this tale as pure legend, without sufficient reason. It is probably true in outline, and it is certain that it took firm possession of the Roman mind. It thus bears witness to the strong Roman feeling of the binding power of an oath, even when given to an enemy; for Regulus had sworn to return if the mission failed.

It took Rome many years and enormous efforts to recover from this disaster, and from the destruction of her fleets by tempests which unluckily followed and gave Carthage once more the mastery of the sea. Carthage, too, had found a man of genius, Hamilcar Barca, whose intense hatred of Rome, ever growing as she gradually prevailed, inspired his people to continue the struggle by sea, and his own forces to hold out grimly in an impregnable fortress in the north-west of Sicily, Mount Eryx, the modern Monte San Giuliano that towers over Trapani. Both sides were exhausted and indeed permanently damaged; but the strength of Rome was more enduring, and in 241 B.C. Hamilcar consented himself to negotiate a peace, by which Sicily and the adjacent smaller islands passed into the hands of Rome for ever. Soon afterwards, taking advantage of a deadly war which Carthage had to wage with her own mercenaries, Rome contrived, in that spirit of 'slimness' already noticed, to get possession of both Sardinia and Corsica. This shows that the Senate understood the importance of these islands for a power in command of the western seas; but unjust dealing brought its own reward. It is possible that the great Hamilcar might have forgiven Rome her injuries to his country but for this. As it was, his hatred of her sunk into his soul more deeply than ever, and that hatred, springing up afresh in the breast of his son Hannibal, all but destroyed his enemy off the face of the earth. He retired to Spain, to organize a Carthaginian dominion there, of which he was himself practically king, and which he destined as a base of operations against Rome in another war; and before he started, as Hannibal himself told the story long afterwards, the father made his boy of nine years old take a solemn oath to cherish an eternal hatred of the enemies of his country.

The plan of invading Italy from Spain was forced upon Hamilcar by the fact that Rome was in command of the sea; it was no longer possible for Carthage to strike at her from Africa without a greater effort to recover that command than her government of merchant princes was now disposed to make. And the fact that Hannibal was actually able to carry out the invasion by land was due to the genius and personal influence of his father in building up a solid dominion in southern Spain with New Carthage (now Cartagena) as its capital. Some historians have thought that of these two extraordinary men the father was the greater; and it is at least true that his was a noble work of construction, while his son's brilliant gifts were wasted in the attempt to destroy the great fabric which Rome had reared in Italy. The attempt was unavailing; the solid Roman structure survived all the assaults of the greatest captain of the ancient world. The glamour of Hannibal's splendid victories must not blind us to the fact that he made two serious miscalculations: he believed that the Italians hated Rome as he did himself, and would join him to crush her; and he hoped, if he did not believe, that Carthage would give him substantial help. Had he judged rightly on the former point, Rome's fate was sealed. But the Italian kinsmen of Rome, who had come to recognize in her their natural leader, never even faltered in their loyalty,[1] and Carthage did but little to help him till it was too late. Thus we have in this terrible war the strange spectacle of a single man of marvellous genius pitting himself against the whole strength of a united Italy with military resources, as we know from the accurate Greek historian, Polybius, amounting to some 770,000 men capable of bearing arms.

Fascinating as we may find Hannibal's wonderful career, much as we may admire his nobility of character, a sober judgement must lead to the conclusion that no great man ever did less for the good of his fellow-creatures. During the fifteen years of his stay in Italy he did irreparable damage to the fair peninsula, and he hardened the hearts of the Romans for all their future dealings with their foes. When at last he left it he was unable to save his own country, and spent his last years in exile, ever plotting against the enemy that had escaped him. A man who is actuated all his life through by a single motive of hatred and revenge can never be reckoned among those who have done something for the benefit of humanity.

[1] With the exception of the southern Samnites, who joined Hannibal after Cannae.

While Hannibal was gaining the loyalty of the southern Spaniards, and organizing their resources, Rome was occupied in trying to extend her power over the Gauls settled in the plain of the Po, and so to make sure of her northern flank, as she had already secured Sicily in the south. But in northern Italy there was no question of gaining the loyalty of the tribes, the Gauls were restless and hostile, and had quite lately made another determined attempt to reach Rome; they actually came within three days' march of the city before they were defeated in a great battle. In 219–218 B.C. Roman armies were still busy in driving roads northward, and planting two colonies, Placentia and Cremona, on Gallic soil and on the Po, when Hannibal descended on them from the Alps. He had countered Roman intrigues in Carthaginian Spain by precipitating a conflict, passed the Pyrenees with an army of nearly 60,000 men, and reached the Rhône before the Senate knew what he was about, and eluded a consular army dispatched to stop him. Scipio, its commander, with true military instinct, sent his army on to Spain, to cut Hannibal's communications with the base he had been preparing so long. This line of communication he never recovered for ten years, and was forced to maintain and recruit his army on Italian soil.

That army, from a purely military point of view, was without doubt one of the best known to history. It consisted chiefly of thoroughly trained Spanish infantry, officered by Carthaginians, and of the best cavalry in the world, recruited from the Numidians of the western region of North Africa. It was one of those armies that can go anywhere and do anything at the bidding of its general, because entire trust in him was the one motive actuating it. It was a professional army, a perfect instrument of war, a weapon admirably fitted to destroy, but without constructive value—with no sap of civilization giving it permanent vital energy. Luckily for Rome, this army had shrunk to very moderate dimensions when it reached Italy; the length of the march, the necessity of leaving some troops in Spain, and the terrible trials of the crossing of the Alps, where the native tribes combined with rock, snow and ice to wear it out, had reduced it to less than 30,000 men.

Yet after a few days' rest Hannibal went straight for the nearest Roman force. This force was now on the north bank of the Po under Scipio, who had returned from the Rhône to Italy. Pushing it back to the new colony of Placentia, where it was joined by that of the other consul Sempronius, Hannibal utterly defeated the combined Roman armies on the little river Trebbia which runs down to that city (now Piacenza) from the Apennines. The Roman power in the plain of the Po was instantly paralysed by this defeat, and the victor at once set himself to organize alliances with the Gallic tribes while he rested and recruited his weary troops. But from the Gauls he got no substantial help; that fickle people had no great reason to welcome an invader when once he was in their territory. And perhaps this was fortunate for him; for if he had marched into central Italy as leader of a Gallic army he would have strengthened, not weakened, the resistance of the whole Italian federation that Rome had so solidly organized. His knowledge of the motives which held this federation together must surely have been seriously imperfect.

But in the spring he crossed the Apennines, and made his way through the marshy and malarious district around the lower Arno, where it is said he

lost an eye from ophthalmia, to meet the consul
Flaminius, who had been sent to cover the approach
to Rome with a large army. Slipping past Flaminius,
Hannibal concealed his army among the hills and
woods on the northern shore of the Lake of Trasimene,
along the western bank of which the railway now runs
on its way from Florence to Rome; and here he lay
in wait for his prey. Flaminius, on a misty morning,
walked into the trap laid for him; his army was totally
destroyed, and he himself was killed. There was now
nothing to stop the conqueror if he chose to march
straight on Rome.

But Hannibal's plans did not include a siege of
Rome; he had brought no siege apparatus, and at no
time during the war did he succeed in getting any from
Carthage, or in making it in Italy. His real object was
to bring the Italians over to his side, to isolate Rome,
and to put a free Italy (so he is said to have phrased it)
in place of a Roman dominion. So he turned his back
on Rome, and made his way at leisure down the
eastern coast of central Italy to the corn-lands of
Apulia, which were henceforward to serve as his chief
base of operations. Hence he might easily reach the
great seaports of Tarentum and Croton, and so get
into touch once more with Carthage, and perhaps, too,
with another power from whom he was already looking
for help, Philip, king of Macedon. But during this
southward march he learnt, apparently for the first
time, that Italy was studded with Roman and Latin
colonies, each a fortress, each provisioned and ready
to resist him: each, too, a miniature Rome, dis-
seminating among the Italians the honour and pride
of Roman citizenship, and the animating spirit of
Italian unity under Roman leadership. One or two
of these fortresses he vainly tried to take, and he must

at this time have begun at last to realize that the mortal hatred of an individual is no match in the long run for the organized vitality of a practical people.

His one chance was to win another great battle, and so to overawe south Italy, to make his base absolutely secure, and to force gradually northward the leaven of anti-Roman feeling on which he calculated. For the rest of that year, 217 B.C., he could not get this chance; the Senate, still cool-headed, had appointed a cool-headed dictator,[1] who knew that his slow and steady citizen soldiers were no good match for a mobile professional army skilfully handled, and steadily refused to accept battle. Not even when Hannibal forced his way northward to the rich plain of Campania, and tried to gain over the wealthy city of Capua, would Fabius be tempted to fight; he dogged the enemy's footsteps, and once tried to catch him in a snare, from which Hannibal escaped by a clever ruse. But next year the Senate dispatched the two new consuls, with an army not far short of 100,000 men, to deal with the enemy in southern Italy; and here, reluctant though one at least of them was, Hannibal enticed them into a battle by seizing a valuable depot of stores at a town called Cannae, near the sea, in the plain of Apulia. Though far inferior in numbers, he contrived by consummate tactics to draw the solid Roman legions into a net, and then used his mobile Numidian cavalry to prevent their escape to the rear. The fight became a butchery, in which 80,000 Romans are said to have fallen. The largest army ever yet sent out from Rome was totally destroyed, and it would seem as if she could no longer escape from her deadly foe.

At this point, the high-water mark of Hannibal's

---

[1] This was Fabius Maximus, who has given his name to the familiar phrase, 'Fabian tactics'.

successes, we may pause to see how the Senate met the news of this most terrible disaster. At no moment in Roman history is the sterling quality of the Roman character and spirit so conspicuously shown. The Senate had to meet not only the immediate military crisis in Italy, but the problems of military and naval policy in Spain, in Sicily, and in the plain of the Po. At home, too, they had to deal with what we may call a religious panic; the people, and especially the women, were beginning to lose nerve, and to fancy that their gods had forsaken them. We can believe the Roman historian when he says that any other people would have been crushed by a catastrophe like this. But the wise men of the Senate simply sat down to repair it, never dreaming of giving in. The city was made safe, fresh legions were enrolled, and thanks were voted to the surviving consul 'for not despairing of the republic'. They would not ransom the prisoners in Hannibal's hands, nor receive the officer whom he sent for this purpose. They were not moved even by the news that southern Italy, the Bruttians, Lucanians, Apulians, and most of the Samnites had joined the enemy, and that isolated towns farther north had deserted them. Capua, the second city of Italy, was betrayed to Hannibal, and he was thus enabled to advance his base from Apulia into the plain of Campania, without leaving an enemy in his rear: but the Senate did not despair. In due time the ranks of this Senate, sadly thinned since the war began, were filled up by a dictator with the best and most experienced citizens available. All possible means were adopted of keeping up the idea of 'the peace of the gods': an embassy was even sent to the great Greek oracle of Apollo at Delphi; the religious panic speedily quieted down. At the beginning of the next year provision was made as usual for the military commands in Sicily, Sardinia, and Spain, and also for a fleet which was being got together at Ostia, the port at the mouth of the Tiber. Within a few months after the battle all was going on in Rome as usual.

So the overwhelming defeat of Cannae did but lead the Romans to victory—to a victory of all the nobler elements in their character over momentary doubt and despair. A people that could recover from that disaster, and go quietly about the work of repairing it, was not likely to be crushed out of existence even by a Hannibal; and though he was to remain as a standing menace for many years on Italian soil, it may fairly be said that henceforward he had no real chance of ultimate success. Two moments of grave anxiety were still to come, but Rome survived them both. One of these was in 211 B.C., when a desperate effort was being made to snatch Capua out of Hannibal's grasp. To induce the Roman government to raise the siege, he made a sudden march on Rome, knowing that no covering army was between him and the capital. He encamped on the Anio, three miles above the city, and rode with an escort of cavalry right up to the gates. But it was all in vain; the Senate had gathered levies amply sufficient to hold the walls, and after plundering the Roman lands Hannibal fell away again, like a sea-wave spent and broken on a rocky shore.

The last moment of extreme peril came four years later, in 207 B.C. The wise foresight of the Senate at the outset of the war had so far secured the Roman hold on Spain, and no reinforcements had reached Hannibal from that source. At last his loyal and able brother Hasdrubal eluded the Roman army there, and by taking a new route—that of Wellington in the Peninsular War—avoided all opposition from the

Romans in northern Spain. Communications with
Italy were now at last open, though not by sea, as they
should have been had the government at Carthage
thrown its whole strength into the work of building
up its naval power afresh. Hasdrubal was forced to
cross the Alps, and this he did with better knowledge
and with less loss than his brother. He made his way
through the Gallic territory and reached Ariminum
(Rimini). Hannibal was in Apulia, where one consul
was holding him in check and dealing with disaffected
Italians; the other was waiting for the invader on the
great coast road south of Ariminum. Hasdrubal sent
dispatches to his brother informing him of his arrival
and suggesting plans of co-operation; but there were
Roman troops everywhere, and the messengers fell
into the hands of the enemy. The consul in the south,
Claudius Nero, thus made aware of the danger, took a
step, without orders from the Senate, which has made
his name for ever famous. He left sufficient force to
hold Hannibal, and slipped away with 7,000 picked
men, without being discovered even by that most wily
of commanders. He marched into the camp of Livius,
the other consul, by night, after a march of some 200
miles, all the loyal people of central Italy feeding and
blessing his army as he went. Two days later the most
decisive battle of the war was fought on the banks of the
little river Metaurus, which runs into the sea from
the Apennines a few miles south of Ariminum. The
Romans were this time completely victorious; the
invading army was utterly destroyed, and Hasdrubal
was killed fighting hard to the last. Nero went swiftly
southwards to his original station, and flung the head
of Hasdrubal—so it was said—into his brother's camp.
For the first time during the long weary years of the
war Rome was mad with joy; and almost for the first

time in her history we note a genuine outburst of gratitude to the gods for this their inestimable blessing. Gratitude, whether to god or man, was not a conspicuous trait in the Roman character; but now, in a moment of real religious emotion, the first thought is one of thankfulness that 'the peace of the gods' is fully restored. It was not only that the Senate ordered a public thanksgiving of three days, but that men and women alike took advantage of it to press in crowds to the temples, the mothers, in their finest robes, bringing their children with them.

The rest of the war-story is soon told. The man who had let Hasdrubal escape him in Spain was a young Scipio, son of a Scipio who had done good work and lost his life there earlier in the war. He himself was a young man of real ability, whose character has always been to some extent a mystery. He was a new type of Roman, one not wholly without imagination, and the long years that he spent in Spain without rivals to check him had perhaps made him cherish and develop his own individuality more than was possible for the staid Roman noble of the old type at home. He believed profoundly in himself, and had the gift of making others believe in him. Returning home the year after the Metaurus battle, he was elected consul, though not yet of the legal age, and had Sicily given him as his province, where after many vicissitudes the Romans were now supreme. He at once proposed to invade Africa, and so to force Hannibal to leave Italy; and the Senate, though they could not or would not risk a large force, gave him leave to make the attempt.

Scipio crossed to Africa in 204 B.C., and ere long the Carthaginian government recalled Hannibal. The great general obeyed, sadly and unwillingly, and in 202 met Scipio in battle near Zama and was beaten;

the undisciplined levies given him by the government were no match for Roman veterans. He himself now advised his people to make peace, and conducted the negotiations, thus doing what he could to make up for the irreparable damage done her in the war by his own implacable hatred of her rival. Carthage was no longer to be a naval power—that was definitely secured by the terms accorded her. She surrendered Spain to the victors, and agreed to pay a large war indemnity by instalments during fifty successive years. Her foreign policy was to be guided by Rome: she could no longer be called an independent State.

So ended the Second Punic War, this great trial of Roman endurance. No people has ever gone through a harder test and survived. The sense of duty and discipline never once failed them; Romans and Italians alike were ready to face death at any moment in defence of their country. But war, always mischievous, when prolonged can sow the seeds of much evil in the future; and we must confess with regret that we are to see but little more of the heroic qualities that had carried Rome through this great struggle.

CHAPTER V

DOMINION AND DEGENERACY

'It was not merely that the disasters of the war had opened the eyes of public men to abuses which had grown up among them; it was not that they hastened to take measures by which such disasters might be prevented from occurring again. Not so much foresight as this was required. The question was at once simpler and more urgently pressing: it was how to prevent the cultivation of the country from falling into a condition of permanent decay. . . . Not only did it become necessary to inquire of political economy what means there were of increasing the wealth of a whole nation at once, but other reforms, less obviously adapted to the immediate need, were now eagerly carried into effect.'[1]

This passage does not refer to Italy and the Roman government after the great war, but to Prussia after she had succumbed to Napoleon and was forced to rest from sheer exhaustion. This rest, skilfully used by statesmen of genius, meant for Prussia recovery, and the opening of a great era of prosperity. If Rome in like manner could have given rest to a weary Italy, and brought all her practical skill to bear on the work of healing and mending, the next two centuries might have been far happier ones for her and for the world. But it is hard for young nations, as for young men, to realize the need of rest, and all the harder in ancient Italy, where fighting had hardly ceased to be looked on as 'the natural industry of a vigorous State'. The Roman Senate was not ripe enough in knowledge of

[1] Seeley's *Life of Stein*, II, 422.

human nature to understand the mischief, moral as
well as material, that a long war can cause, especially
if the enemy has been in your country harrying and
devouring, no one knowing when his turn will come
to be ruined. And, indeed, we may doubt whether
even if Rome's leading men had been able to understand the nature of the mischief, they would have had
the skill to discover and apply the necessary remedies.

This mischief and its results must be the subject of
this chapter, for without getting some idea of it we
cannot understand the perils to which civilization was
exposed in the next two hundred years by Roman
degeneracy, or the way in which they were eventually
overcome. But I must just glance, to start with, at
the policy actually pursued by the Senate in the period
following the war, which placed Rome in the position
of arbiter of the whole Mediterranean world, and
mistress of a territory many times as large as Italy.

The two recent invasions of Italy by formidable
enemies must have taught the Senate the necessity of
making it impossible that there should be another.
But another might yet be looked for—so at least they
believed—not from Spain or Africa, but from the
great military power of Macedon. Philip of Macedon
had been among Rome's enemies since Cannae; but
not even Hannibal could persuade him to attack her
with vigour, and he missed his chance. Roman
diplomacy had stirred up the Greeks against him, and
he had plenty to do at home. But no sooner was
Carthage crushed than the Senate coaxed the tired and
unwilling people into declaring war against him, and
this led in the course of the next half-century to the
overthrow of the Macedonian kingdom, and finally
to its absorption into what we must now begin to call
the Roman Empire. At the same time, Rome acquired a

protectorate over the whole of Greece, at first honestly meant to defend her against Macedon, but destined to pass rapidly into dominion. The Greeks in their leagues and cities were never again really free. If they could have kept from quarrelling among themselves, they might have endured this protectorate with profit; but ere Rome had done with them they were to feel her heavy hand.

Thus the 'peasants of the Tiber' became masters of the Balkan peninsula as well as of that of Italy. In the same period they completed the conquest of Italy up to the Alps, not without difficulties and defeats, and went on driving their roads and planting colonies in all parts. In the Spanish peninsula, from which the Carthaginians had been finally driven, they now established two permanent commands (*provinciae*), one in the basin of the Ebro in the north-east, and the other in the fertile valleys of the Guadiana and Guadalquivir, as the two great rivers of southern Spain are now called. From these they slowly but persistently, after their manner, and in spite of many defeats and even disgraces, pushed up into the high tablelands of central Spain, until they had brought the greater part of the peninsula under their sway. Here they had to deal with a people very different from the weary and exhausted Greeks and Macedonians; a people only half civilized, but lively, intelligent and capable of making excellent soldiers, as Hannibal had found. It is to the credit of the Romans that, in spite of much cruelty and misgovernment, they gave this peninsula a real civilization, of which the traces are still abundant especially in the south, and a beautiful language, which descends directly from their own.

In order to maintain their communications with Spain by land as well as by sea, they also had to look to the coast between the western Alps and the Pyrenees. Here they made a lasting alliance with the ancient and flourishing Greek colony, Massilia (Marseilles); and in defending Massilia from the attacks of mountain tribes they were gradually drawn into the acquisition of a permanent hold on the lower valley of the Rhône. This, again, in due time very naturally became the starting-point for fresh advance into the heart of modern France. No one who has seen the Rhône from Lyons to Marseilles can resist the conclusion that a power in possession of its lower reaches must inevitably advance along it northward.

There is yet a fourth peninsula in this land-locked sea, known for want of a better name as Asia Minor, which juts out from the Asiatic continent, and forms a meeting-place for Eastern and Western civilizations. This was in the last three centuries B.C. the fighting-ground of the successors of Alexander the Great, kings of Macedon, Pergamum, Syria and Egypt, who wasted the vigour of humanity in wars that to us seem needless. The Romans were soon drawn into a war with the king of Syria, an ally of Philip of Macedon, and won a great victory in this peninsula in the year 190 B.C. But they annexed no territory here until the last king of Pergamum left his kingdom to Rome by will some sixty years later. The Senate preferred to act as arbitrator, to make alliances, to reward friendly states, to use diplomacy rather than force; and on the whole they succeeded. Their policy was often tortuous, sometimes even mean, but in the long run it did more good than harm to humanity that a young and virile people should interfere among these monarchies.

Thus, whether we look west or east in the Mediterranean, we find the Roman power predominant everywhere within eighty years from the end of the war with Hannibal. It is not easy to explain in a few words what drove this power onwards. It was not simply the commercial motive, as with Carthage. It was not simply the desire to conquer and annex, for the Senate was slow to undertake new duties of government abroad if their object could be attained in some other way. But what was that object? Undoubtedly it was self-defence to begin with; but self-defence, once successful, only too easily slips into self-assertion. This self-assertion, as we see it in Roman policy, is perhaps the natural result of victorious wars upon a growing, robust and disciplined people. It may be compared with the determined self-assertion that governed German policy in recent generations, but with this difference—that the Romans never twisted their consciousness of strength and superiority into a racial theory. No Roman senator had a doubt that his people were the strongest and most competent to control the world, but he recognized the right of other peoples to exist and to use their language and customs and traditions. Still, the constant assertion of this proud conviction brought many suitors and suppliants to Rome, whose presence flattered Roman pride, and whose diplomacy sometimes involved the government in new wars, giving ambitious consuls their opportunity of increasing the fame and the wealth of themselves and their families. So in due time there arose a dominion of the following military commands or provinces: one in Sicily, one in Sardinia, two in Spain, one in southern Gaul, one in Macedonia with Greece attached to it, one in Asia Minor, and one in Africa, after the destruction of Carthage by her old enemy in 146 B.C. Of the method of governing these provinces I will say something in another chapter. Now let us try to estimate some of the results of these continuous wars in distant parts, taken together with the long struggle with Carthage. We shall find a change in every department of the people's life, and in almost all a change for the worse.

First, let us look at that family life which formed the essential fibre of the old body politic, and provided the most powerful factor in the Roman character. We have but to think of the immense numbers of citizens killed or captured in war, or carried off by the pestilences that always follow war, to see what paralysis of family life there must have been. Fathers and grown-up sons innumerable never came home at all; and long service far from home would, in any case, deprive the family of the natural influence and authority of its head. Mothers might do much to fill up the gap, and the tradition of the dignified and righteous Roman lady was not as yet wholly weakened; but there were signs that the women in this period were getting steadily more excitable, more self-asserting, more luxurious. It is in this age that divorce begins to make its appearance, a sure sign of the decay of the old family life. There were rumours, too, of the poisoning of husbands by their wives, and on one occasion two noble ladies were put to death for this crime by the verdict of a council of relations. In an extraordinary attempt to introduce into Italy the exciting orgies of the Greek religion of Dionysus, women were among the most prominent offenders. The changing position of women at this time is illustrated by a famous saying of Cato, that 'all men rule over women, we Romans rule over all men, and our wives rule over us'.

With the decay of the old family life, the wholesome training of the children in manly conduct (*virtus*) and sense of duty (*pietas*) could not but suffer, too. Old-fashioned families would keep it up, but among the

lower classes it was hard to do so owing to bad housing
and crowding in the city; and in the noble families
there was undoubtedly a change for the worse, though
we know of one or two great men of this age who took
pains with the moral as well as the intellectual training
of their boys.[1] For a people controlling the Mediterranean world it was necessary to educate the mental
faculties, and more especially to teach a boy to speak
and read Greek, which was the language of half the
civilized world, and the language of commerce everywhere. Now Rome could not supply teachers for this
kind of education; Romans were not competent, nor
would they have condescended to such work. The
Greeks were the one people who could undertake
what we call the higher education, and they were now
beginning to swarm in Rome. Some Greek teachers
were free men, but the greater number were slaves
captured in the wars; and thus the first requisite in a
schoolmaster, that he should be looked up to and
willingly obeyed, was too often absent in this new
education. It is men, not methods, that really tell in
education. In his heart, as we know from many
striking passages in Roman literature, the grown-up
Roman despised the Greek of his time, and we may be
sure that the Roman boy did too. Greek literature and
rhetoric, now fast becoming the staple of the higher
education, could never make up for the lack of moral
discipline. If we find a spirit of lawlessness in the
coming age, and a want of self-restraint in dealing with
enemies or opponents, we shall not be far wrong in
ascribing it in great part to the loss of the wholesome
home influence, and to the introduction of an education

[1] Plutarch's *Lives* of Cato the Elder and Aemilius Paullus,
which can be read in a translation, will give examples of this
better type of education.

outside the home, which entirely failed to make up for the decay of the simple old training in duty and discipline.

The fact is that the Romans were now coming under the influence of a new idea of life, in which the individual played a more important part than ever before at Rome. The Roman of the past had grown up modelled on a type and fixed in a group, so that the individual had little chance of asserting himself; but now we find him asserting himself in every direction, and in every class of society. To think for oneself, even in matters of religion; to speak from personal motives in the senate or law courts; to aim at one's own advancement in position or wealth—all this seemed natural and inevitable to the men of that day. And so by degrees the individual became the mainspring of action instead of the State. There were some noble exceptions, but most of the leading men played their own game, and often won it at the expense of the State. Many a general hurried on operations towards the close of his command so as not to be superseded before he could earn a triumph, and pass in splendid procession up to the temple on the Capitol, with chained captives following his chariot. And the small men became more and more unwilling to serve as soldiers in distant lands, and more and more rebellious against discipline. In little more than half a century after Hannibal had left Italy the Roman armies were beginning to be incapable of their work.

Along with this too rapid growth of the individual, we have to take account of the sudden incoming of wealth and growth of capital. The old Roman family group had no capital except its land and stock. But now, as the result of plunder and extortion in the provinces, most men of the upper classes had some capital in money, and this was almost always invested in public works and State undertakings of all kinds, e.g. the raising of taxes and the fitting out of fleets and armies. These things were all done by contract, and the contracts were taken by companies, in which every man was a shareholder who had anything to invest. Thus the inflow of wealth brought with it the desire of making money, and the forum of Rome became a kind of stock exchange in which the buying and selling of shares was always going on, and where every man was trying to outwit his neighbour. Of a really productive use of capital in industry or commerce we hear very little; and it would seem that the Roman of that day had no idea of using his means or opportunities in ways likely to produce well-being in the world.

If we turn to rural Italy, the prospect is hardly less dreary. Incalculable damage had been done to agriculture in the great war, and agriculture, in the broad sense of the word, was almost the only Italian industry. Corn, wine, oil, wool and leather had formerly been produced in sufficient quantities to keep the inhabitants in food and clothing, each community growing what it needed, as in medieval England. But this simple form of agricultural economy must have suffered a severe shock, not only from the ravages of armies, but from the decrease of the working population owing to war and pestilence.

In order to restore a decaying industry you must have the men to work at it. Depopulation as the result mainly of war was a disease epidemic in the Mediterranean in this age; and in Italy we know for certain how rife it was, for we have the records of the census of the body of Roman citizens, which show a steady falling-off in this period, and we must suppose that the same causes were at work among the non-Roman population of the peninsula. There was, indeed, a remedy, but it was almost worse than the disease—I mean the vast numbers of slaves now available for labour. The unskilled slaves, captured or kidnapped in Spain, Gaul, Epirus, Thrace or Asia Minor, were cheap in the Roman market, and would do well enough to run a farm with, especially if that farm were chiefly a pastoral one, with flocks and herds needing no great experience or skill to look after. This cheapness, and the physical conditions of rural life in a mountainous country, made cattle-running and sheep-tending a profitable industry. Large districts of Italy, especially in the centre and south, became covered in this period with huge estates owned by capitalists, and worked by rough and often savage slaves, who were locked up at night in underground prisons and treated simply as 'living tools'. No ray of hope ever broke in on these miserable beings; no free citizen gave a thought either to their condition or the economic danger of the system; philanthropy and political economy were unknown in the Roman world, for imagination and reflection were alike foreign to the Roman mental habit.

Even on the estates of moderate size which were not entirely pastoral, slave-labour was the rule. We know something of such a farm from the treatise on agriculture written by Cato at this time, which has come down to us entire; and it is plain from what he says that though free labour might be employed at certain seasons, e.g. at harvest, the economic basis of the business was slave-labour. There is no doubt that all over Italy the small farm and the free cultivator were fast disappearing, with the rapid growth of capital and the cheapness of slaves. In the city of Rome, now beginning to harbour a vast population of many races, the number of domestic slaves tended constantly to increase; they were employed in every capacity by men of wealth and business. Many of them were cultivated men, Greeks for example, who could act as clerks, secretaries or teachers, and these had a fair chance of earning their freedom in time; but great numbers were low and vicious beings, who had no moral standard but that of obedience to a master, no moral sanction except punishment.

Thus, though the shrinkage of the free population was evil enough, the remedy for it was even worse. The slave, plucked up by the roots from the soil in which he had flourished in his native land, deprived of family, property, religion, must in the majority of cases become a demoralized and hopeless being. In the plays of Plautus, the great writer of Latin comedies, who lived during this period, the slave is a liar and a thief, and apparently without a conscience. For the slave-owner, too, the moral results were bad enough, though not so obvious at first sight. A man who is served by scores of fellow-creatures who are absolutely at his mercy is liable to have his sense of duty gradually paralysed. Towards them he has no obligations, only rights; and thus his sense of duty towards his free fellow-citizens is apt to be paralysed too. A habit of mind acquired in dealing with one set of men naturally extends itself and affects all human relations. And so the Roman character, naturally hard enough, came in the later days of the Republic to be harder than ever. In our next two chapters we shall meet with unmistakable proofs of this. Incredible cruelty, recklessness of human life, callousness in dealing with the vanquished and the subject peoples, meet us at every turn in that dark age of Mediterranean history. Under the baleful influence of slavery the hard Roman nature had become brutalized; and we have to wait for the Christian era before we find any sign of sympathy with that vast mass of suffering humanity with which the Roman dominion was populated.

We must glance in the last place at the change brought about by the wars in another department of Roman life, viz. in the working of the constitution. The reader will remember that in early Rome the salient feature in that constitution was the *imperium* of the magistrate, just as in private life the salient feature was the discipline of the family under the rule of the head of the household. The man who held the *imperium* was irresistible so long as he held it, though a wise custom made it necessary for him to seek the advice of his council, the Senate, on all questions of grave importance. But now the long wars took the consul and his *imperium* away from the city for long periods, and as the Empire began to grow up and include provinces beyond the sea, those periods became longer and longer. There were, indeed, always two magistrates with *imperium* in Rome, the praetors, who for long past had been elected yearly to help the consuls in judicial business; but the prestige of their *imperium* never reached the level of that of the consuls. And even when a consul returned home, though the majesty of the *imperium* was present in his person as ever, it was not his hand that was really on the helm. The decision of great questions did not lie with him, but with his council, whose knowledge of affairs and whose 'courage never to submit or yield', had carried Rome safely through a long series of unexampled trials.

In the period after the war with Hannibal, the Senate, not the *imperium*, is clearly the paramount power in the working of the constitutional machinery. To take a single instance: when the people declined to sanction the war with Philip of Macedon, the Senate directed the consul to convince them that they were wrong, and both consul and people bowed to its will. They had other agents in the tribunes of the people, if the consuls failed them, and would now and then even coerce a consul by means of the power of the tribune. But what chiefly gave the Senate its power was the fact that it was the only permanent part of the government. A senator held office for life unless ejected by the censor for immorality, while all the magistrates were elected for a year only. In the Senate there sat for life every man who had held high office and done the State good service, and as there were some three hundred of these, it was almost impossible for the yearly holders of *imperium* to resist their deliberate judgements. And for those judgements the Senate was responsible to no man.

Probably no assembly has ever comprised so much practical wisdom and experience as the Roman Senate of this period; but that wisdom and that experience was limited to the working of the constitution, the control of foreign affairs, and the direction and supply of armies. As has already been hinted, when it came to providing remedies for economic and moral evils such as I have been sketching, the senators were useless; they had no training in the art of the State physician, and no desire to learn how to diagnose disease. They were almost all men of the same type, and with the same public and private interests. They belonged, in fact, to a few noble families, and new blood was seldom to be found in their ranks; for though they had all at one time or other been elected to office by the people, the choice of the people almost always fell upon members of the old tried families.

The principle that the son of a family that has done good service to the State will be likely himself to do such service seems to have taken firm hold of the mind of the Roman voter; and thus it came about that the Senate, in spite of its great capacity for business, gradually became an *oligarchical* body— the mouthpiece of one class of society. The principle is by no means a bad one in some stages of social growth, but it is sure in the long run to produce the vices as well as the virtues of oligarchy—the dislike of any kind of change, the narrow view of social life, the want of sympathy with other classes and of the desire to understand their needs. We shall see in the next two chapters how these oligarchical weaknesses brought the Senatorial government to an ignominious end. It had saved the State from its deadliest enemy; it had laid the foundations of the Roman Empire; but it failed utterly when called on to do the nobler work of justice and humanity.

This aptly brings us to our last point in this chapter. As the Roman oligarchy stood to the people, so Rome herself stood as an oligarchy to the populations of her Empire. The Roman citizen was the one most highly privileged person in the civilized world of that day. The great prize of his citizenship was not, as we might suppose it would be, the right to vote in the assemblies, to choose magistrates and pass or reject laws, nor the right to hold office if elected, for to that distinction very few could aspire; it was really the legal protection of his person and his property wherever he might be in the Empire. No one could maltreat his person with impunity; a fact well illustrated in the life of St. Paul (Acts xxii. 25 foll.). He could do business everywhere with the certainty that his sales, purchases, contracts would be recognized and defended by Roman law, while the non-citizen had no such guarantees for his transactions. No other city in the Mediterranean had a citizenship to compare with this in practical value, for the Roman law was gradually becoming the only system of law with a real force behind it. To live a life of security and prosperity you must be a Roman citizen.

We, in these days of comparative enlightenment, might perhaps imagine that with a gift like this citizenship in their hands the Romans would have been quick to reward their faithful Italian allies, who had served in their armies all through these wars, by lifting them to their own level of social and political privilege. But if so, we should be ascribing to the human nature of Roman times a degree of generosity and sympathy which was, in fact, almost unknown. We might fancy that they would have grasped the fact that their old city-state had outgrown its cradle, that Italy and not the city of Rome now really supplied the force with which the world was ruled, and that they would put the Italians on the same level of advantage as themselves, at least as regards the protection of person and property. But after the war with Hannibal the tendency was rather in the other direction. All allied Italian cities continued to have to supply contingents to Roman armies and fleets; yet Rome offered them no privileges to make up for these burdens, and her magistrates got more and more into the habit of treating them as inferiors. The Latins, too, that is the old cities of the Latin league, and the colonies with Latin *right*, as it was now called, who already had some of the privileges of citizenship, were carefully prevented from acquiring more, from becoming full citizens of Rome. In this exclusive policy, which seems to us mean and un-grateful, the Roman government undoubtedly lost a great chance, and had to pay dearly later on for her negligence.

The fact was that the imperial idea had taken hold of the governing Romans with a force to which that of our British 'imperialism' cannot compare for a moment. They were so busy governing, negotiating, arbitrating and making money, that the condition and claims of their own city and country failed to attract the attention of any but a very few among the educated aristocracy. Depopulation, decline of agriculture, slavery and its accompanying evils, injustice to the Italian allies and the ever-growing discontent occasioned by it, misgovernment and plunder in the provinces, all these sources of mischief were now accumulating force, and were before long to bring the whole Roman system to the brink of ruin. But Rome on the brink of ruin meant civilization in imminent danger; for no other power could any longer withstand the barbarians of northern Europe, who were even now beginning to press down into sunny southern lands. So it is that the story of the succeeding century, the last before the Christian era, is one of the most thrilling interest. How did Rome survive and overcome these dangers with renewed strength, and succeed in organizing an Empire on the firm foundations of law and justice, destined to hold the barbarians at bay long enough to inspire them with profound respect for the civilization they were attacking? This question we shall try to answer in the remaining chapters of this book.

CHAPTER VI

THE REVOLUTION: ACT I

ENOUGH was said in the last chapter to show that the age we are now coming to, the last century before Christ, was one full of great issues not only for Rome, but for all Western civilization. The perils threatening, both internal and external, were so real as to call for statesmen and soldiers of the highest quality; and as we shall see, this call was answered. It was this century that produced most of the famous Romans whose names are familiar to us: the two Gracchi, Marius, Sulla, Pompey, Cicero, Caesar, and finally Augustus, all of whom helped in various ways to save Italy and the Empire from premature dissolution. It was, in fact, an age of great personalities, and one, too, in which personal character became as deeply interesting to the men of the time as it is even now to us. For as the disciplinary force of the State waned, the individual was left freer to make his own force felt; and so great was that force at times, that we are tempted to fix our attention on the man, and to forget the complicated motives and interests of the world in which he was acting. Undoubtedly we should be wrong in doing so; for a very small acquaintance with the facts would show us these great men struggling incessantly with difficulties, and carried out of their own natural course by adverse currents. But none the less it is true that hardly any other period of history shows so much, for good and evil alike, depending on individual character. So as the last chapter dealt mainly with perils and problems, our next two will be occupied with the efforts of these famous men to meet the perils and solve the problems.

Depopulation and the decline of agriculture were the first of the perils to be considered seriously. This was done in the year 133 B.C., not by the Senate, whose business it really was, but by a young and enthusiastic noble, in some ways one of the finest characters in Roman history. Tiberius Gracchus had the right instinct of the old Roman for duty, and for a Roman he had an unusually tender and generous nature; but he had not the experience and knowledge necessary for one who would take this difficult problem in hand, which in our day would be prepared for legislation by careful inquiry about facts, conducted by authorized experts. His education had been mainly Greek, and a study of hard facts did not form a part of it.

Still, he was able to enlist the help of some capable men, and produced and finally carried a bill which may be called a Small Holdings Act. No one was henceforward to hold more than 500 *jugera* (about 300 acres) of *public land*, or if he had sons, 250 more for each of two. Public land was land owned by the State, but occupied by private men who paid (or ought to have paid) rent for it in some form. Land owned as well as occupied by private men could not be touched; but there was abundance of the other, for the State had retained its hold on a large part of the land of Italy acquired by Rome. This land was now to be divided up in allotments, the State retaining its ownership and forbidding sale, a futile attempt to keep the settlers on the land, even against their will. This courageous plan for bringing the people back to the land was put in action at once, and we still have a few of the inscribed boundary stones set up by the commissioners chosen to carry it out. And there is reason to believe that it did some good in regard both to depopulation and agriculture. The Senate made no serious attempt to interfere with it when once it was passed, and it continued in force for many years.

But unluckily the Senate had done all it could to prevent the bill passing; they would have nothing to say to it, and they put up a tribune to veto it. The veto of the tribune of the plebs was an essential part of the constitution, and could not be disregarded; but Gracchus, also a tribune, had but one year of office, and if he could not get his bill through during that year, he must give up the attempt for a long while. Enthusiasm got the better of prudence; he deliberately broke with law and usage; he defied the Senate and its prerogative, and he carried a bill deposing the tribune who acted for the Senate. He also proposed to offer himself as a candidate for re-election, contrary to the custom if not the law of the constitution. With the highest motives he thus laid himself open to the charge of making himself master of the State, by violating the custom of its forefathers (*mos maiorum*). It had always been a maxim of Roman law that the man who aimed at tyranny might be slain by any one; and now that even the best aristocrats believed Gracchus guilty, this was the fate that overtook him. He was killed on the Capitol, and the cowardly rabble made no attempt to save him.

The story is perhaps the saddest in Roman history. A little more patience and practical wisdom, a little more of the spirit of compromise on either side, might have saved the situation. The old Roman discipline had avoided violence, and got over constitutional difficulties by consent; now Gracchus laid a violent hand on the constitution, and was repaid with violence by its unworthy defenders. Intending only reform, he ended with starting revolution.

There was another enemy within the gates beside depopulation, one not less to be feared, but less easy to realize as an enemy; I mean slave-labour. Gracchus may be pardoned for making no direct attempt to attack it, though just before his tribunate there had been a rising of slaves in Sicily which showed the military as well as the economic danger of the situation. It is said that 200,000 slaves were in rebellion there at one time, and the war was only ended after a long struggle. These risings, more of which followed at intervals, and finally a most formidable one in Italy sixty years later, were symptoms of a disease calling for a very skilful physician; but no physician was to be found until Caesar tried to make a beginning. As yet the Romans had not had time to realize this danger; living in an atmosphere of slave-labour, they believed that they throve on it. And as this was in one sense true, owing to the decrease of the free labouring population, the evil was too subtle for an uncritical people to discern. In spite of all these dangerous risings, there is no sign in the copious literature of this last century of the Republic of any consciousness of the poison at work.

Nine years after the murder of Tiberius Gracchus, his younger brother Gaius, elected tribune, took up his work and went far beyond his designs. In this most interesting and able man we come at last upon a Roman statesman of the highest order; a practical man, no mere idealist of the new Greek school, and yet a man of genius and a born leader of men. We possess a picture of him, evidently drawn from the life by one who knew him, which shows these gifts at a glance.[1] When he was at the height of his activity, busy with a multitude of details, he seems to have given that eyewitness the impression that he was almost a monarch. But a close study of all we are told about him seems to prove that he was in reality one of those rare men, like Caesar later on, who profoundly believe that they can do the work needed by the State better than any other man, and who are justified in that belief. He would see to the carrying out of his own measures with astonishing speed, sparing no pains, amazing even his enemies by the unflagging energy with which he worked, and by the way he contrived to get work out of others. Perhaps the secret was that he was a gentleman in the best and noblest sense of that word; for Plutarch says that in his dealings with men he was *always dignified, yet always courteous*, invariably giving to every man his due.

In fact, the personality of this man is the real explanation of his work. If it had been possible for him to retain that personal influence which Plutarch emphasizes, and to keep his legislative power even for a few years, as a modern statesman may expect to keep it, it is quite possible that Rome might have escaped an era of danger and degeneracy. But that could not be. A triple-headed Cerberus was guarding the path that led to effectual reform: the forms of the old constitution, out of date many of them, and unsuited to the needs of a great empire: the narrow spirit of the oligarchical faction, opposed, for self-regarding reasons, to all change: and lastly, the mean and fickle temper of the mongrel city populace, whose power was sovereign in legislation and elections. In the effort to overcome

[1] In Plutarch's *Life* of him, especially chapters v and vi, where Plutarch is plainly reproducing the evidence of an eyewitness.

this Cerberus Gracchus lost his precious personal influence, and found his original designs warped from their true bearing. He survived through two tribunates, in the course of which he did much valuable work, but in the third year he was brutally and needlessly slain by his political enemies. Already Rome had put to death two of the most valuable men she ever produced, and in the coming century she was to put to death many more.

He had begun his work by a noble effort so to mend the constitution that a reformer might be able to pass his laws without breaking it, as Tiberius had been tempted to do. He tried to increase the numbers of the Senate, so as to leaven that great council, which he rightly looked on as the working centre of the constitution, with new ideas and wider interests. And he sought, too, to solve the great problem of citizenship, by giving the Italians some effectual share in it, and so at least the chance of making their voice heard in Roman politics. But for such measures of real progress neither Senate nor people were ready: the Senate was the stronghold of old prejudices, and the people were not pleased to admit Italians to its privileges. Both these great projects, which show how far-reaching Gracchus's views as a statesman were, proved complete failures.

To conciliate the Senate became more and more hopeless as Gracchus lost his personal influence, and he gave up the attempt. Instead, he dealt the senatorial oligarchy a heavy blow by depriving senators of the right to sit in judgement on ex-provincial governors accused of extortion (a crime now becoming only too common), and giving it to the class below, the Equites, or men of business. Thus he made a split between the two upper classes of society, which had very unfortunate results. Not less unhappy was another measure, meant to conciliate the hungry free population of the city, on which he must depend for the passing of his laws. There had long been a difficulty in feeding this population: for its number had increased beyond all expectation, the corn-supply was not properly organized, and the price of grain was constantly fluctuating. Recognizing the fact that any legislator was in peril who could not make it impossible that the price should rise suddenly, he fixed a permanent price, lower than had often ruled at Rome, to be maintained at State cost, whether or no the State were a loser. But here he went too far, and gave later and less scrupulous demagogues the chance of making still more serious mischief. No doubt he thought that the State need not be a loser, if production, transport, warehousing and finance were organized as he meant to organize them; but there is also little doubt that he was mistaken, and that henceforward the 'people' were really being fed largely at the expense of the State, and lapsing into a condition of semi-pauperism.

I have said enough to show how sad was the failure of the first real statesman produced by Rome. Yet Gracchus was able to do some useful work which survived. Under his auspices was passed a great law, of the text of which we still possess about one-third, for the trial of provincial governors accused of extortion: and we know of another, bearing his own name, which regulated the succession to these governorships with justice and wisdom. Also he took up his brother's land bill, and carried it on with that practical persistency which is reflected, as we saw, in Plutarch's *Life* of him. But in spite of high aims, and some successes, his story is a sad one; and the loss to Italy and the Empire at that moment of a man of righteous aims and practical genius was simply incalculable.

Whatever else the Gracchi did, or failed to do, they undoubtedly succeeded, both in their lives and in their deaths, in shaking the power and prestige of the senatorial government; and nothing had been put in its place, nor had it even been reformed. Henceforward for a long period there was no constitution that could claim an honest man's loyalty or devotion; the idea of the State was growing dim, and the result was inefficiency in every department. The governing class was corrupt and the army undisciplined, and this at a time when there was coming upon Rome, and upon the civilized world, a period of extreme peril from foreign enemies. This corruption and inefficiency became obvious a few years after the death of the younger Gracchus in a long struggle with a Numidian chief, called Jugurtha, in the province of Africa, who contrived to outwit and defy Roman envoys and Roman armies, by taking advantage of the corruptibility of the one and the indiscipline of the other. Luckily for Rome this war produced a great soldier in Gaius Marius, a 'new man' of Italian birth, and another in L. Cornelius Sulla, a man of high patrician family; and these two, though destined to be the bitterest foes, brought the war to a successful end.

But a far greater peril was threatening Italy herself. As we look at the map of Italy, or better still (if we have the chance) as we look up at the huge rampart of the Alps from the plain of the Po, we are tempted to think of this great barrier as impenetrable. But mountain ranges are always weak lines of defence, and history, ancient and modern alike, has abundantly proved that Italy is open to invasion from the north.

Hannibal and his brother had pierced the western flank of the range, where later on there were regular thoroughfares between Rome and her western provinces; and at the eastern end, where the passes gradually lessen in height, access was easy into Italy from the north-east. Beyond this mountain barrier, at the time we have now reached, there was much disturbance going on: hungry masses of population were moving about in search of fertile land to settle in, themselves pressed on by other peoples in the same restless condition. In 113 B.C. a great migrating host, apparently of Germans, but probably gathering other peoples as it advanced, seemed to threaten the weak point of the eastern Alps.

A consul with an army was in Illyria, and tried to stop them in the country now called Carinthia, but was badly beaten. If there had been a man of genius at their head, the enemy might have penetrated into Italy; as happened again just a century later, there was nothing to stop them between the Alps and Rome. But the great host was not tempted, and pursued its way westward. In 109 they suddenly appeared beyond the western Alps, where they destroyed another consular army, and yet another fell before the Gauls of that region. Then in 105, at Orange, in Roman territory, while trying to cover the road to Massilia and so into Italy, the Romans experienced a defeat almost as terrible as that of Cannae, and half the Empire lay open to the victors. But once again they left their prey untouched, and passed westwards in search of easier conquests.

Rome had a breathing-time of nearly three years, and she also had the right man to save her. Marius remodelled the army, revolutionizing it in equipment, tactics, and discipline. For material he was driven hard, and had to find recruits as best he could, drawing them from all parts of the Empire: but he had time to drill them into fine soldiers, and to lay the foundation of a marvellously perfect human defence for Mediterranean civilization. The result was one great victory near Marseilles, and another at the eastern end of north Italy, into which the barbarians had at last penetrated: and Italy was once more secure.

Now we have to see how this peril, or rather the effort made to escape it, led to changes of the most far-reaching character in the Roman power and polity. Italy had not been saved by Roman armies or the Roman government, but by Marius and the army which he had created. For five successive years Marius was consul, contrary to all precedent, away from Rome; and the army he created looked to him, not to Rome, for pay, promotion, and discharge. We may call that host of his a Mediterranean army under the command of an Italian. It was far more like Hannibal's army than like the old Roman citizen armies that had won the supremacy in Italy; it was a professional army devoted to its general, but with little thought of the Roman State whose servant he was. And henceforward, until Augustus restored the sense of duty to the State, the Roman armies, excellent now as fighting machines, and destined to secure effective frontiers for the Empire, were the men of Marius, Sulla, Pompey, Caesar, and a constant source of anxiety and danger for the State which they were supposed to serve.

This 'long-service army' brought Rome face to face with another difficulty, and led indirectly to another great peril. When the soldiers returned home after many years of service in distant regions, what was to be done with them? Many, perhaps most of them, had no homes to go to. The veterans might naturally demand some permanent settlement, but the Senate showed no sign of appreciating the problem, and in this matter the general was helpless without the Senate. So it happened that many of them lapsed into the crowded city, to pick up a living we know not how, with the help of the distribution of cheap corn. Among them were beyond doubt numbers of non-citizens, who could not legally vote in elections or legislation, and were inadequately protected in regard to person and property, in spite of all the long service they had gone through. These men began to offer themselves as voters, and to exercise the rights of citizenship illegally; yet the confusion of the registers was such that they could not be detected. At last the adulteration of the Roman citizen body became so obvious that the consuls of 95 B.C. passed a law with the object of making it clear who was a citizen and who was not, and of eliminating those who were not really privileged.

But it was now too late to take such a step. News of it spread over all Italy, and it was construed as a deliberate attempt to exclude Italians from the citizenship. Five years later another vain attempt was made by a noble tribune to do as Gracchus had wished to do, to extend the citizenship and to enlarge the Senate: but he was assassinated before his laws were passed, and then at last there followed the inevitable outbreak, perhaps long meditated. The social war, as it is called, in reality a civil war, was a crisis in the history of European development. When it was over, the ancient city-state of the Greeks and Italians had vanished in Italy, and in its place arose a new form of polity, for which there was then no name.

The sturdy peoples of central Italy entered on the

desperate venture of setting up a rival power against
Rome: a plan which, if successful, would have
paralysed Rome's work in the world whether for good
or evil. They chose the city of Corfinium, in the heart
of the Apennines, some hundred miles east of Rome,
gave it the new significant name Italica, and made it,
as Washington is now, the city-centre of a federation,
where deputies from the various members should
meet and deliberate under the presidency of consuls.
But now was seen the value of the strategical position
of Rome. She could strike in any direction from inner
lines, while safe from attack or blockade by sea; but
Corfinium had no such natural strategic advantage,
nor any unifying power. Yet the Italians were for
some time successful in the field, and Rome was for a
whole year in the utmost peril. At the end of that year
(90 B.C.) the Etruscans and Umbrians to north and
east showed signs of joining the confederates, and then
for the first time Rome was likely to be put on the
defensive, with enemies on her left flank, as well as
on her right and in front. So a law was hastily passed
giving the precious citizenship to all who had not
taken up arms; and this was the beginning of a process
by which, in some few years, the whole of Italy became
Roman in the eye of the law, while, on the other hand,
it might be said not untruly that Rome became Italian.
Henceforward we have to think of the whole peninsula
as forming the material support of Mediterranean
civilization.

With this great change one might have expected
that peace and harmony would return to Italy. But,
on the contrary, she is now about to enter on the most
terrible time that she has ever known; even her
miserable feuds of the late Middle Ages never quite
reached the horror of those of Marius and Sulla.

It is hard to explain this; but looking back at what was said in the last chapter about the causes of demoralization, it is possible to make a guess. We have to think of a vast slave State, worn out in the struggle with dangers within and without, enfeebled by constant warfare, and now given over into the hands of powerful military masters, with hosts of veterans at their beck and call. The State seemed to have lost its claim to loyalty, even to consideration: and in its place were rival generals, leaders also of political factions—in these years two, Marius the self-seeking champion of the Italians and the Roman plebs, and Sulla the self-seeking champion of the old aristocracy. All principles were lost on either side in the intensely bitter hatred of the parties and the personal rivalry of the leading men. It happened that a war was threatening in the East, of which we shall hear more in the next chapter; and the command in this war, the great prize of the moment, became a bone of contention outweighing all interest of the State.

The prize fell to Sulla; but no sooner was his back turned on Italy than the Marian faction fell on their political enemies and sought to destroy them by wholesale murder. Compromise was utterly forgotten; all the brutality of unbridled human nature was let loose. And when Sulla returned from the East, after driving the enemy out of Roman territory, the massacres were revenged by more massacres. The loss to Italy of many thousands of her best men, and among them scores who might have done good work in the world, was a calamity never to be repaired.

Where, one may ask, was the old Roman *gravitas* and *pietas*, the self-restraint and sense of duty that had won an empire? It would seem as if the capacity for discipline were entirely lost, except in the long-service army. But the mere fact that in the army this survived is one not to be neglected, even if it were exercised less on behalf of the State than in the interest of the individual commander. For if there could be found a statesman-soldier who could identify himself with the true interest of the State, and so bring back not only the army, but the people, to a right idea of Rome's position and duty in the world, the Empire and civilization might yet be saved. Without the army these could not be defended; and the one thing wanting was to make the army loyal to the State as well as to its general. Only the general himself could secure this loyalty, by making himself the true servant of the State.

But the man into whose hands Rome had now fallen was one who could not possibly identify himself with the best interests of the State, because an unsympathetic nature had denied him the power of discerning what those interests were. Sulla has been compared to Napoleon, and in one or two points the comparison holds good; but the two were utterly unlike in the main point, the power of sympathetic discernment. Napoleon, cruel and unscrupulous as he often was, showed plainly, when he organized the institutions of France, or Switzerland, or Egypt, that he understood the needs of those nations: he divined what would enable them to advance out of stagnation to some better form of life, social and political. But Sulla, though he saw that the call of the moment was for order at almost any price, for peace, strong government, and reform, went about his work in a way which proved that he did not delight in it, or care for the people for whom he was legislating. He did what was necessary for the moment, but did it with force ill concealed under constitutional forms. So no wise man rejoiced in his work, and the Roman people as a whole felt no loyalty towards him. He provided in many State departments an excellent machinery, but not the motive force to work it.

Nothing in history shows better how much in remedial legislation depends on the spirit in which it is undertaken. Sulla saw that the great council, the Senate, must be the central point and pivot of government, unless indeed there were a master at hand, like himself, to undertake it; that the popular assemblies, untrained in discussion and affairs, could not do the work of administration. Though the theory of the constitution had always been that the people were sovereign, he contrived that the Senate, which had so long practically governed under an unwritten constitution, should now rule without let or hindrance on a basis of statute law; and here we see an unwritten constitution growing into a written one. By a great law of treason, the first on the Roman statute-book, he made it almost impossible to defy the Senate without the risk of political effacement.

This may be called reactionary, but under the circumstances it was not a reaction to be complained of. The pity was that this master legislator had really none to be grateful or loyal to him but his own army and followers. His constitutional legislation was for the most part swept away soon after his death, and there was no one to lament. On the other hand, all that he did that was not strictly political, and in particular his reorganization of what we may call the civil service, and of the criminal law and procedure, was so obviously progressive and valuable that no one ever attempted to destroy it; and some of his laws of this kind held good throughout Roman history.

Sulla attained his power in 81 B.C., resigned it in

79, and died next year at his villa on the warm Campanian coast, where he had gone to enjoy himself in self-indulgence and literary dilettantism. Here he wrote that autobiography of which some few fragments have come down to us in Plutarch's *Life* of him— a life which will repay the reader, even in translation. One of these fragments has always seemed to me to throw real light on the man's strange nature, and on the imperfection of his work. 'All my most happy resolutions', he wrote, 'have been the result, not of reasoning, but of momentary inspiration.' In other words, Sulla did not believe in thinking over a problem, and herein he was a true Roman. He hoped to do the right thing on the spur of the moment. Thus it was that no one ever knew what he would do; no one could trust him nor believe in him. Like so many in that and succeeding ages he believed profoundly in Fortune: he called himself Sulla the Fortunate, and gave like names to his two children. What exactly he meant by Fortune we cannot say; but we may be sure that it was no such conception of a power ruling the world as might guide a statesman's feet out of the path of self-seeking into a more bracing region of high endeavour.

CHAPTER VII

THE REVOLUTION: ACT II

WITH the death of Sulla ends what we may call the first act of the Roman Revolution. We are now in the middle of a revolution in more than one sense of that word. The constitution and the government of Rome are being slowly but surely changed, and at the same time the era of the free and independent city-state of the Graeco-Roman world is being brought to an end. Both these changes, as we can see now, were inevitable; without them the civilized world could not have been defended against barbarian invasion, or Italy united into a contented whole possessed of Roman citizenship. In the first act, as I have called it, the immediate danger of invasion was checked, both in north and east, and Italy had become Roman, enjoying perfect equality with Rome under the great body of Roman law now being rapidly developed.

But, in truth, this inevitable work of change was not as yet half done. It was soon found that both in north and east some definite system of frontier must be fixed, or the Empire would be in continual peril from without. It was also found that Sulla's constitution would not work, and that to defend the frontiers of civilization effectively there must be a government of sterner force, whatever form that force might take. Thus in the second act of the Revolution we have two main points to attend to: first, the settlement of the frontiers against Oriental despots and wandering hordes of Germans: secondly, the acquisition of power by a great soldier-statesman, Julius Caesar, and the abandonment, as a working power, of the ancient polity of Senate and people. And inasmuch as this period of revolution was also the age of the best and purest bloom of Latin literature, I must find space later for a few words about Cicero, Lucretius and Catullus.

I said in the last chapter that there was a very dangerous enemy threatening the eastern or Greek part of the Empire. This was Mithradates, king of Pontus, that part of Asia Minor which borders on the Euxine (Black Sea) eastwards: a man of genius and ambition, and by no means to be reckoned a barbarian. It is curious that he began his great career by protecting Greek cities against their enemies, and one is tempted to ask whether he might not have been at least as beneficent a champion and master for the Greek world as Rome herself. But we must look at things with Roman eyes if we are to understand the work of Rome in the world; we must think of Mithradates as the Romans then did, as the deadly enemy alike of Greek freedom and of Roman interests.

His armies had invaded Greece in 87 B.C. and had even occupied Athens, while the Greek cities of Asia Minor had willingly submitted to him: the whole Hellenic world was fast coming under his sway. Then Sulla had expelled his generals from Greece proper, and had forced him to accept such conditions of peace as kept him quiet for a few years. But when Sulla was dead he started on a fresh career of conquest, and once more the Roman protectorate of Greek civilization was broken down. For a time it looked as if no power could restore it. The sea was swarming with pirates from Cilicia, who constantly harassed the Roman fleets, and ventured even as far as Italy, snapping up prisoners for sale as slaves in the great slave-market at Delos. And behind Mithradates and these pirates there was another power even more formidable. Tigranes, king of Armenia, had also been extending his dominions southward, and was even in possession of Syria and Judea at the time of which we are now speaking, 75 B.C. Should the two kings unite their forces and policy, it would be all but impossible for Rome to remain the mistress of the eastern Mediterranean and the Hellenic world. It was another example of Rome's wonderful good fortune that this alliance was never solidly effected till too late.

The Senate, left by Sulla to govern the world, soon showed that it was incapable of grasping the necessity of vigorous action in the east. It was not till 74, four years after Sulla's death, that they sent out a really capable general with an adequate force. Lucullus, whose name has become a byword for wealth and luxury, was in his prime a soldier of great ability, and he soon broke the power of Mithradates, who immediately fled for refuge to Tigranes. This made it absolutely necessary to deal with that king also; and Lucullus invaded Armenia and captured the king's new capital, Tigranocerta. Unluckily, he had not that supreme gift of a great commander which enables him, as it afterwards enabled Caesar, to lead his men where and when he will; the army mutinied, refusing to go farther into the wild Armenian mountains, the most distant and formidable region a Roman army had as yet penetrated. Lucullus had to retreat.

Then, under pressure from the men of business who were losing money by the instability of Roman dominion in Asia, Senate and people agreed to supersede Lucullus by a younger man, reckoned the best soldier of the day, and a military pupil of Sulla. This was the famous Gnaeus Pompeius, known to us familiarly as Pompey. In 67 he had been commissioned to clear the sea of pirates, and did it effectually. Now, with a combination of civil and military power such as no Roman had yet enjoyed, he took over Lucullus's army, made short work of Mithradates, and utterly broke up the empire of Tigranes. He overran Syria, the region between the Mediterranean and the desert stretching to the Euphrates, penetrated to Judea and took Jerusalem. This famous event is the first in the long and sad story of the relations of Rome and Judea. At Jericho, before he reached the Holy City, he received the dispatch which told him of the death of Mithradates, the removal from the scene of one who had been for thirty years Rome's most dangerous enemy.

The result of the efforts of Lucullus and Pompey was the establishment of a frontier system in the East which may be said to have held good for the rest of Roman history. The principle of it is not easy to explain; but if the reader will take a map and trace the river Euphrates from its sources in western Armenia to the Arabian desert, and then make it clear to himself that all within that line was to be either Roman or under Roman suzerainty, he will be able to form some idea of its importance in history. There were to be three new Roman provinces: Pontus with Bithynia in the north of Asia Minor, Cilicia on its south-eastern coast, and Syria, the coast region from Cilicia south-wards to the frontier of Egypt. But between these and the Euphrates there were two kingdoms, Cappadocia and Galatia, and other smaller ones, which formed *a Roman sphere of influence* where Rome herself could not as yet be constantly present. Imperfect as this system seems, it was quite strong enough to spread the prestige of the Roman Empire far and wide in the East, and the great king of Parthia, beyond the Euphrates, might well begin to be alarmed for his own safety.

Now in settling this frontier system Pompey had, of course, to attend to an infinite number of details, and to make decisions, convey privileges, negotiate treaties, and grant charters, in dealing with those cities new and old which formed a most important part of his plan of settlement and defence. All this had to be done on his own responsibility, but would need the sanction of the Senate to be recognized as legally valid. When he returned home in 62 B.C. he expected that the Senate would give this sanction, especially as he had just disbanded his army, with which he might, if he had chosen, have enforced his claims. But the Senatorial government was reduced to such a state of imbecility that the majority would have nothing to do with Pompey's invaluable work: they were jealous, they were lazy, and, above all, they were ignorant. So he had to fall back after a year or two on the consul of 59, C. Julius Caesar, who undertook to get the necessary sanction from the people if not from the Senate. In return Pompey was to help him to get a long command in Gaul, so that the work of frontier defence there begun by Marius might be resumed and completed. At this very moment a German people, the Suebi, whose name still survives in the modern Swabia, were threatening the rich plains of what is now eastern France: and then, just as a peace had been patched up with them, a Gallic tribe, the Helvetii, suddenly issuing from its home in (modern) Switzerland in search of new settlements, or pressed on by other tribes beyond it, was about to break into the Roman province of Transalpine Gaul. But Caesar had now done his part by Pompey, though not, indeed, without straining the constitution; and moving with the wonderful swiftness that afterwards became characteristic of him as a general, he reached

Geneva just in time to stop them, and soon afterwards beat them in a great battle and forced them back to their homes.

This was the beginning of a career of conquest which made the glorious country we know as France into the most valuable part of the Roman Empire, and later on into the most compact and gifted nationality in Europe. What motives inspired Caesar in all he did during the nine years he spent there we need not ask, for we can only guess the answer; though he has left us his own story of his campaigns in simple straightforward Latin, he has not chosen to tell us what was all along at the back of his mind. Ambition, says the superficial historian; the desire to make himself in due time master of Rome and the Empire. But we may take it as certain that Caesar, a man whose health was never strong, would not have exposed himself to constant peril of his life for nine successive years had he really all the time been nursing a secret ambition which death or serious illness might at any time destroy. What he really seems to have loved, like C. Gracchus, was work—steady, hard work with no one to hinder him, and with a definite practical object before him. Doubtless further hopes or fears were in his mind, but this great practical genius, with an intellect characteristically Roman,[1] though more scientific in its tendency than that of any other Roman known to us, was always bent on the work immediately in front of him, and never rested till it was completed to his satisfaction.

When Caesar hurried north to check the Helvetti in 58 B.C. there was but one Roman province in Gaul, the south-eastern part of modern France (which still teems with Roman remains and inscriptions), together

---

[1] He came of an old Roman patrician family.

with a considerable district to the west of it at the foot of the Pyrenees. When he finally left Gaul at the end of 50, the whole of modern France and Belgium had been added to the Empire, though not as yet organized into provinces. He did not take long to reach our Channel and to subdue the tribes on the coast; he began the written history of our island by invading it twice, and recording such information as he could gain about its geography and inhabitants. He crossed the Rhine into Germany by a bridge constructed for him by his engineers: in siegecraft he could employ all the devices of ancient military science, assault-towers, sapping and mining; and the speed of his movements was proverbial. The Gauls were doubtless amazed at these performances, as he meant them to be; and, after one heroic effort to save themselves from becoming an appendage of a Mediterranean empire, they had to submit. While we can sympathize with these noble efforts for freedom, or blame Caesar for what sometimes seems unnecessary cruelty, we must remember that from this time forward the country from the Rhine to the ocean becomes a great factor in European civilization.

There was still, indeed, a gap in the line of frontier; how was the eastern end of the Alps to be protected from invasion? There, as we saw, the great rampart was lowest, and beyond it the barbarians were an unknown quantity. Here the river Danube eventually became the frontier, and was carefully connected with that of the Rhine; but this completion of the great work had to wait for half a century, and in the meantime luckily no inroad was made or threatened. It was Tiberius, afterwards emperor, another great soldier, with an army almost as devoted to its general as that of Caesar, who after long steady effort planted the

Roman power firmly in this region (pp. 132–3). From a military point of view the Roman Empire, and therefore Western civilization as a whole, owed its very existence for centuries to Pompey, Caesar and Tiberius, with their splendidly trained armies and their skilful engineers.

This great and enduring feat of conquest and settlement was not the work of the State, or due to the old civic sense of duty and discipline; it was the work of the armies, due to their good discipline, and to their loyalty to their leaders. This being so, it was of course only natural that the armies and their leaders should claim to control the action and policy of an enfeebled State, as Sulla had already claimed it. This is really, put in a very few words, the secret of the Roman imperial system that was to come; so, too, in England, in Cromwell's time, the State passed into the hands of the army, because that army (though in our case but for a short time) represented the best instincts and purposes of the nation. But the question of the moment was whether the commander of one of these Roman armies could so identify himself and his soldiers with the State and its true interests, as to become the means of establishing a sound and efficient government for the Mediterranean world. Sulla had failed so to identify himself: he had neither knowledge enough nor sympathy enough. The chance had been open to Pompey when he returned from the East in 62, but he had disbanded his army and declined it; he was in many ways a valuable man, but he was not the stuff that real statesmen are made of. After the long war in Gaul the chance was open to Caesar, and he accepted it without hesitation.

He accepted it, but in truth he had to fight for it. For years his operations in Gaul had been looked on at

Rome with suspicion, especially by a clique of personal enemies led by the famous Cato, a descendant of the old Cato whom we met in the previous century. These men looked on Caesar as dangerous to the State—and dangerous indeed he was, to that old form of State which neither they nor he could make vigorous and efficient. They clung to the worn-out machinery of the constitution, to the checks, the vetoes, the short tenure of office, to the exclusive right of the Senate to deal with the ever-increasing administrative business of the Empire. Knowing, or guessing, that Caesar, like Gaius Gracchus, would force his personal will on the State if he judged it necessary, they were determined to prevent his becoming a political power, and they brought Pompey to the same view, and armed him with military force to be used against Caesar—against the man, that is, who had spent the best years of his life in indefatigable work for the Empire and civilization. The result was civil war once more; civil war that might unquestionably have been averted by a wider outlook, a more generous feeling, a spirit of compromise, on the part of the high aristocrats who, like Cato, believed themselves to be struggling for liberty. The liberty they were struggling for was in reality the liberty to misgovern the Empire, and to talk without acting efficiently.

It is plain, as we may learn from the abundant correspondence of the time,[1] that they did not know the man they had to deal with. Caesar took them completely by surprise; in a few weeks he had cleared Pompey and Senate and their army out of Italy, had provided for the government, and gone off to Spain to secure the West by turning the Pompeian armies out of that peninsula also. After a brilliant campaign of

[1] See below, p. 119.

H

six weeks, admirably described by himself in his work on the Civil War, he forced those armies to surrender and then let them go unhurt, as he had done just before in Italy. His clemency took the world by surprise as much as his generalship.

But the worst was not over for him. Pompey was gathering all the resources of the East against him, and concentrating them in Epirus with a view to the reconquest of Italy. Again Caesar's rapidity saved him; he was just in time to strike the first blow by crossing the sea from Brindisi—a rash expedient—and hampering Pompey before his concentration was effected. Here, however, in his eagerness to bring the campaign to an issue, he made a serious blunder, and had to pay for it by defeat and a retreat to the corn-growing plain of Thessaly. Pompey unwisely followed him, instead of invading Italy; and here, in August 48, was utterly beaten at the battle of Pharsalia. The worn-out old soldier fled to Egypt, where he was treacherously murdered by one of the king's generals. He was an estimable man with many excellent qualities, and in a more tranquil age might have well become what Cicero wished to see him, the presiding genius of the Roman State.

Caesar had yet much war before him—war in Egypt, in Asia Minor, in Africa and in Spain, against the supporters of the old régime, for nothing he could do in the way of conciliation would persuade them to forgive him the crime of seeking to identify himself with the State. In doing so they deprived him of the time which he might have spent to far better purpose at Rome on the work of efficient government. As it was, he had been able to spend but a few months in all at home, when on March 15, 44 B.C., he was murdered at a meeting of the Senate, at the feet of Pompey's statue, by a small group of assassins, some of whom were intimate friends of his own. They thought he was on the point of assuming a visible despotism, and they had some justification for the suspicion, though it was probably a delusion. To kill a tyrant, they thought, was to do a noble work in true old Roman fashion. So did the murderers of the Gracchi.

From what little we know about such work of reform as Caesar had time for, we may take it as certain that these deluded assassins made a sad blunder. Caesar's legislative work was fragmentary, but every item of it shows intelligence and political insight. He did not attempt to turn out a new constitution in black and white; he did the work of government mainly himself for the time being, and we do not know how he meant to provide for it after his death. In the most important matter of all, the adjustment of the Empire to the home government, and especially the subordination of the provincial governors to a central authority, he forestalled the imperial system of the future: he made himself the central authority, to whom the governors were to be responsible. The other most important question of government, that of the power and composition of the Senate, he answered by raising the number of senators to 900, as Gaius Gracchus had wished to do, and thus destroying the power of the old narrow oligarchical cliques. But perhaps his practical wisdom is best seen in his economic legislation for Rome and Italy. He was the first statesman to try and check the over-abundance of slave-labour: the first, too, to lay the foundation of a reasonable bankruptcy law. He regulated the corn-supply in the city, and brought down the number of recipients of corn-doles to less than one-half of what it had lately been. Again, he laid down general rules for the qualification of candidates for municipal office in Italy, and arranged for the taking of a census in all the cities every five years, the records of which were to be deposited at Rome. It would seem as if he meant to work out the enfranchisement of Italy to its natural conclusion: for he not only completed it by extending it to the Alps, which had never yet been done, but went beyond the bounds of Italy, offering the citizenship freely both to Gauls and Sicilians.

It may seem strange, but it is perhaps some measure of Caesar's influence on history, that historians have disagreed, and still disagree, in their judgement of his personality. As we have his own military writings, a life by Plutarch, a few letters written by or addressed to him, and innumerable allusions to him in contemporary literature, we ought to be able to form some just idea of him. As one who has been familiar with all these materials, and many others of less value, during the greater part of a lifetime, I say without hesitation that Caesar was the one man of his time really gifted with *scientific intelligence*—with the power of seeing the facts before him and adjusting his action to them. This intelligence, combined with great strength of will, made him master of the Roman Empire; and though his character was by no means perfect, he seems to have used his mastership, not like a capricious Oriental despot, but with a real sense of responsibility. A man who combines the qualities of an intelligent statesman in bad times with a generous temper, good taste and good scholarship, surely deserves to be thought of as one altogether out of the common. In Shakespeare's picture of him, derived from Plutarch's biography, and representing only the last two days of his life, he seems weak in body and overweening in spirit, and is probably meant to seem so by the dramatist for his own purposes. But no sooner have the murderers done with him than the true greatness of the man begins to make itself felt, and is impressed on us in page after page to the end of the play, of which the action may be said to be pivoted on the idea of the horror and the uselessness of their deed.

So far in this chapter and the last I have been treating of this age as one of action. It is indeed filled full of human activity, in spite of the laziness of the governing class as a whole. But this activity was shown not only in war and politics; this is also an age of great poets and real men of letters. I must say a word about the two greatest poets, Lucretius and Catullus; but among the men of letters there stands out one far above the rest whose life and genius it would take a long chapter to explain. Cicero's pre-eminence is not easy to understand even after long study of his voluminous works: yet I must try to make it clear that he was, in fact, one of the greatest of all Romans.

Of Lucretius it is our fate to know nothing except his poem in six books on 'The Nature of Things'. But his name is Roman, and the poem has the true Roman characteristic of being essentially practical in its object. That object will seem a singular one to those who are unacquainted with the Greek and Roman culture of this age. What roused a poet's passion in this man's mind was simply the desire to free others, as he had freed himself, from the fetters of superstition, or, as he calls it, *religion*; to make them abandon the delusive dream of a life after death, to repudiate the old stories of torment in Hades, and all foolish legends of the gods, who in his view took no interest whatever in human life. All this was, of course, derived from Greek philosophy, the doctrine of the Epicurean school, but no Greek had ever put such passion into a creed as Lucretius. His poetry at times almost reminds us of the grandeur and authority of the Hebrew prophets, so ardently did he believe in his own creed, and in his mission to enforce it on others. Uncouth and dry as much of it is—for he has to explain that Epicurean theory of the universe known still to science as the atomic theory—he breaks out now and again into strains of magnificent verse which reveal a mind all burning within. Here is a specimen: it must be in prose, for no verse translation seems adequate—

'What hast thou, O mortal, so much at heart, that thou goest such lengths in sickly sorrows? Why bemoan and bewail death? for say that thy life past and gone has been welcome to thee, and that thy blessings have not all, as if they were poured into a sieve, run through and been lost without avail: why not then take thy departure like a guest filled with life, and with resignation, thou fool, enter upon untroubled rest? But if all that thou hast enjoyed has been squandered and lost, and if life is a grievance, why seek to make any addition, . . . why not rather make an end of life and travail? for there is nothing which I can contrive or discover for thee to give pleasure: all things are ever the same (iii. 933 foll.).'

The other poet, Catullus, was not of Roman birth, but, like so many literary men of this and the following age, an Italian from the basin of the Po. He had no practical aim in writing poetry: he simply wrote because he could not help it, about himself and his friends and his loves. It was his own self that inspired him chiefly, and it is still himself that interests us. According to his own mood, now fresh with the happiness of an artist, now darkened by anger or self-indulgence, his poems are exquisite or repulsive; but they are always true and honest lyrics, and interesting because they are so full of life and passion. Catullus is one of the world's best lyric poets. Here is one of his gems—

> Is aught of pleasure, aught of solace sweet
> Permitted, Calvus, to the silent grave,
> What time the tale of sorrow we repeat,
> Yearning o'er memories we fain would save?
>
> Know this. From Love and Friendship if a tear
> Can make its way into that silentness,
> Quintilia feels untimely Death less drear,
> For hearing of the love that still can bless.
>
> CATULLUS, xcvi. (by s. t. i.).

Lastly, we come to the man of letters who has given his name to this period of literature, which indeed draws more than half its interest from him and from his works. Marcus Tullius Cicero was an Italian, and had little of the Roman character in his make; he came from the town of Arpinum, among the foothills of the Apennines some sixty miles south-east of Rome. He made his way into Roman society by his social and conversational powers, and by his capacity for friendship, and into the field of politics by his great gift of oratory, which was now indispensable for public men. As a 'new man' he never was really at home with the high aristocracy, but he was a man of many friends for all that, and reckoned among them all the great men of his time, including both Caesar and Pompey. His best and truest friend, who worked for him all his life with unsparing care, was a man of business who stood outside of politics, Pomponius Atticus; and of Cicero's letters to this faithful friend and adviser nearly four hundred survive to prove the reality of that life-long devotion. Some five hundred letters to and from other correspondents are also extant, and the whole collection forms the most fascinating record of a great man's life and thoughts that has come down to us from classical antiquity.

In modern times Cicero has often been treated with contempt by scholars as a shallow thinker, deriving all his inspiration from Greek originals, and as a feeble statesman, brilliant only as an orator. It is true that there is a want of *grit* in much that Cicero wrote: he was the child of his age, never tired of writing and talking, little used to profound thinking, and rarely acting with independent vigour. But he has two claims on the gratitude of posterity which should never be forgotten. First, he made Latin into the most perfect language of prose that the world as yet has known. The echoes of his beautiful style can be heard centuries afterwards in the Latin fathers of Christianity, especially St. Augustine and Lactantius, and they are still audible in the best French and Italian prose-writers of to-day. Secondly, of all Romans Cicero is the one best known to us as an individual human being: and few indeed who have had the chance to become really familiar with him can fail to love him as his own friends loved him. He was not the stuff of which strong statesmen are made; he was too dependent on the support and approval of others to inspire men with zeal for a cause—especially for a losing cause. His own consulship in 63 B.C. was brilliant, for he was able to combine the best elements in the State in the cause of order as against anarchy—anarchy which threatened the very existence of Rome as a city; and at the end of his life he showed the same ability to use a strong combination to good purpose in the political field. But he was not of such strong growth as to mark out a line of his own, and at some unhappy moments of his life his weakness is apt to move our pity, if not our contempt.

But with all his weak points Cicero is one of the best and greatest of all Romans. His gifts were rich, and he used them well. We know him as a man of pure life in an impure age, and as one who never used his gifts or opportunities to do harm to others, whether political enemies or helpless provincials. We know him, too, as a faithful husband and a devoted father. And lastly, we know that he was not lacking in courage when the assassin overtook him—the last of a long list of great men of that age to die a violent death.

CHAPTER VIII

AUGUSTUS—THE REVIVAL OF THE ROMAN SPIRIT

THE death of Julius Caesar seemed to plunge the world once more into darkness. We have evidence enough of the general feeling of horror and despair that overwhelmed men, of the fear of civil war, of never-ending rivalries, when no man's life or possessions would be safe from injustice and factions. Power fell into the hands of a far more unscrupulous man than Caesar, the Mark Antony of Shakespeare's play; but he had a rival in Caesar's nephew and adopted son, afterwards known as Augustus. Civil war, of course, followed: first, war between these two and the murderers of Julius, and then war between the two victors. Antony, who had in a division of the Empire taken the eastern half, and married Cleopatra, the ambitious queen of Egypt, was crushed at the naval battle of Actium: the Empire became once more united, and hope began to spring up afresh.

Instead of following the melancholy history of these years (44 to 31 B.C.) let us try to realize the need of a complete change in men's minds and in the ways of government, if the Roman Empire was to be preserved, and Mediterranean civilization with it. We can best do this by learning something of the two men who more than all others brought about the change: Virgil, the greatest of Roman poets, and Augustus, the most fortunate and discerning of Roman statesmen. Augustus began a new system of government, based, no doubt, on the ideas of Julius, which lasted, gradually developing itself, till the fifth century of our era. Virgil, the poet of the new Roman spirit, kept that spirit alive into the Middle Ages, and rightly read, he keeps it still before us.

If Virgil had lived in an ordinary age, when the flow of events was smooth and unruffled, he might have been a great poet, but hardly one of the world's greatest. But he lived in a crisis of the history of civilization, and he was called to do his part in it. For a century before he wrote, the one great fact in the world was the marvellous growth of the Roman dominion. When he was born, seventy years before the Christian era, Rome was the only great civilized power left, and a few years later it looked as if she had not even a barbarian rival to menace her, except the Parthians far away in the East. The Roman was everywhere, fighting, trading, ruling; nothing of importance could be done without the thought—What will Rome say to it?

Yet just as Virgil was growing to manhood it became obvious, as we have seen, that this great power was in reality on the verge of breaking up. She had abandoned justice and duty, and given herself to greed and pleasure. Her government was rapacious: she was sucking the life-blood of the nations. She had lost her old virtues of self-sacrifice, purity of family life, reverence for the divine. The rulers of the world had lost the sense of duty and discipline; they were divided into jarring political factions, and had felt the bitterness of civil war, in which men killed each other in cold blood almost for the sake of killing. But with Julius Caesar's strong hand and generous temper it must have seemed to many that a better time was coming, and among these was the young poet from Mantua under the rampart of the Alps.

No one who knows Virgil's poems well can have any

doubt that all his hopes for himself and his family, for Italy and the Empire, were bound up with the family of the Caesars. The sub-alpine region in which he was born and bred had been for ten years of his boyhood and youth under the personal rule of the great Julius, and had supplied him with the flower of that famous army that had conquered first Gaul and then the world. It is possible that the poet owed his position as a Roman citizen to the enlightened policy of Caesar. Even now we cannot read without a thrill of horror the splendid lines in which he records the eclipse of the sun and the mourning of all nature when the great man was murdered by so-called patriots.[1] With such patriots, with the rapacious republican oligarchy, he could have had no sympathy, and there is not a trace of it in his poems. When, during the civil wars that followed the murder, he was turned out of his ancestral farm near Mantua to make room for veteran soldiers, he owed the recovery of it to the master of those soldiers, the second Caesar, whom henceforward he regarded not only as his own protector and friend, but as the one hope of the Empire.

Now this younger Caesar, nephew and adopted son of Julius, though not a great soldier or a hero in any sense, was yet one of those rare men who learn wisdom in adversity, and use it to overcome passion and violence in themselves and others. He came gradually to see that Italy and the world could not be rescued from misery and despair by war and strong government alone. He grasped the fact, which Sulla had missed, that the one thing wanting was loyalty—loyalty to himself and belief in his mission: loyalty to Rome and Italy, and belief in their mission in the world. Confidence in him, and in the destiny of Rome, might

[1] *Georgics*, I, 463 foll.

create in men's minds a hope for the future, a new self-respect, almost a new faith. Divided and depressed as they were, he wanted to set new ideals before them, and to get them to help him loyally towards the realization of those ideals. Economically, morally, religiously, Italy was to rise to new life in an era of peace and justice.

This may seem too grand an ideal for a man like Augustus Caesar, who (as I have said) was no hero, and who certainly was no philosopher. But it is none the less true that he understood that 'peace hath her victories no less renowned than war': and that his own conviction, based, perhaps, on shrewd political reasonings, inspired his poets and historians to hail a new age of peace and prosperity. In one way or another they all fell in with his ideas. Their themes are the glory and beauty of Italy, the greatness of Rome, the divine power which had given her the right to rule the world, and the story of the way in which she had come to exercise that right. But as Virgil is the greatest figure in the group, so is his *Aeneid* the greatest work in which those ideas are immortalized. The Roman Empire has vanished, the ancient city, which rose in fresh magnificence under Augustus, has crumbled away; but the *Aeneid* remains the one enduring monument of that age of new hope.

It is said that Augustus himself suggested to the poet the subject of the *Aeneid*. If so, it was characteristic of a man who used every chance of extending his own fame and influence without forcing them on the attention of his people. If a poem was to be written on the great theme of the revival of Rome and Italy, Augustus himself could not of course be the hero of it, nor even Julius: political and artistic feeling alike forbade. But a hero it must have, and he must be placed, not in the burning light of the politics of the day, but in the dim distance of the past. Such a hero was found in the mythical ancestor of the Julian family, Aeneas, son of Venus and Anchises. A legend, familiar to educated Romans, told how this hero, who is mentioned by Homer as one of the great Trojan warriors, wandered over the seas after the fall of Troy, and landed at last in Italy; how he subdued the wild tribes then dwelling in Latium, brought peace and order and civilization, and was under the hand of destiny the founder of the great career of Rome. His son Iulus, whose name the Julii believed themselves to bear, was in the legend the founder of the city from which Rome herself was founded; and thus the family of the Caesars, the rescue of Italy from barbarism, and the foundation of the Eternal City, might all be brought into connexion with the story of Aeneas the Trojan. Here, then, was the hero, the type of which the antitype was to be found in Augustus.

This is how the *Aeneid* became a great national and a great imperial poem. It created a national hero, and endowed him with the best characteristics of his race, and especially with that sense of duty which the Romans called *pietas*: this is why it became a great national poem. It connected him with the famous stories of Greece and of Troy, and made him prophetically the ancestor of the man who was rescuing the Empire from ruin: this is why it became a great imperial poem. The idea was a noble one, and Virgil rose to his subject. Though the *Aeneid* has drawbacks which for a modern reader detract from the general effect, yet whenever the poet comes upon his great theme the tone is that of a full organ. Even in a translation the reader, though he cannot feel the witchery of Virgil's magic touch, may recognize and welcome the recurrence of that great theme, and so learn how its treatment made the poem the world's second great epic. It instantly took a firm hold on the Roman mind; it came to be looked on almost as a sacred book, loved and honoured as much by Christian Fathers as by pagan scholars. Italy has given the world two of the greatest poems ever written: the *Aeneid* of Virgil, and the *Divina Commedia* of Dante, in which the younger poet took the imaginary figure of his predecessor as his guide and teacher in his travel through the scenes of the nether world.

But we must now leave poetry for fact and action, and try to gain some idea of that work of Augustus which laid the solid foundation of a new imperial system; a system of which we moderns not only see the relics still around us, but feel unconsciously the influence in many ways. Augustus had found time to discover, since the death of Julius, that the work to be done would fall mainly into two great departments: (1) Rome and Italy must be loyal, contented, and at peace; (2) the rest of the Empire must be governed justly and efficiently. To this we must add that the whole must contribute, each part in due proportion, to its own defence and government, both by paying taxes and by military service.

1. The city of Rome, with a population of perhaps half a million, of all races and degrees, had been a constant anxiety to Augustus so far, and had exercised far more power in the Empire than such a mixed and idle population was entitled to. He saw that this population must be well policed, and induced to keep itself in order as far as possible; that it must be made quite comfortable, run no risk of starvation, have confidence in the good will of its gods, and enjoy plenty

of amusement. Above all, it must believe in himself, in order to be loyal to his policy. When he returned to Rome after crushing Antony and Cleopatra, the Romans were already disposed to believe in him, and he did all he could to make them permanently and freely loyal. He divided the city into new sections for police purposes, and recruited corps of 'watchmen' from the free population; he restored temples and priesthoods, erected many pleasant and convenient public buildings (thus incidentally giving plenty of employment), organized the supply of corn and of water, and encouraged public amusements by his own presence at them. He took care that no one should starve, or become so uncomfortable as to murmur or rebel.

But, on the other hand, he did not mean this motley population to continue to have undue influence on the affairs of the Empire. True, he gave them back their free State (*respublica*), and you might see magistrates, Senate, and assemblies in the city, just as under the Republic. But the people of the city had henceforth little political power. The consuls and Senate were indeed far from idle, but the assemblies for election and legislation soon ceased to be realities. In elections no money was now to be gained by a vote, and in legislation the 'people' were quite content with sanctioning the wisdom of Augustus and his advisers. At the beginning of the next reign it was possible to put nearly the whole of this business into the hands of the Senate, and the Roman people made no objection. Seeing that they were only a fraction of the free population of the Empire, it was as well that this should be so; the rest of the citizen body could not use their votes at a distance from Rome, and the Senate and the *princeps* [1] (as Augustus and his immediate successors

[1] See below, p. 134.

were called) represented the interests of the Empire far better than the crowd of voters.

Of the work of Augustus in Italy we unluckily know very little, but what we do know shows that he worked on much the same principles as in the city. Italy was made safe and comfortable, and was now free from all warlike disturbance for a long period. Brigandage was suppressed: roads were repaired: agriculture and country life were encouraged in all possible ways. A book on agriculture written even in Augustus's earlier years boasts of the prosperity of rural Italy, and Virgil's poem on husbandry is full of the love and praise of Italian life and scenery. Here is a specimen—

> But no, not Medeland with its wealth of woods,
> Fair Ganges, Hermus thick with golden silt,
> Can match the praise of Italy . . .
> Here blooms perpetual spring, and summer here
> In months that are not summer's; twice teem the flocks:
> Twice does the tree yield service of her fruit.
>
> .   .   .   .   .   .
>
> Mark too her cities, so many and so proud,
> Of mighty toil the achievement, town on town
> Up rugged precipices heaved and reared,
> And rivers gliding under ancient walls.[1]

2. The peaceful state of Rome and Italy made it possible for Augustus to undertake, in person to a great extent, the more important work of organizing the rest of the Empire. He found it a motley collection of provinces, principalities, tribes and cities, with little organic unity; he left it a strongly compacted union of provinces and dependent kingdoms grouped around the Mediterranean, which for a long time to come served two valuable purposes. First, it protected Mediterranean civilization against barbarian attack, the most valuable thing done for us (as I said in my first

---

[1] From James Rhoades's version.

chapter) by Roman organization. Secondly, it gave free opportunity for the growth of that enlightened system of law which has been the other chief gift of Rome to modern civilization. And also, though without any purpose on the part of the government— nay, in spite of distrust and occasional repression—it made possible the rapid growth of Christianity, during the next half-century, which seized on the great towns and the main lines of communication to spread itself among the masses of the people.

Augustus was able to do all this work beyond Italy quite legally, and as a servant of the State. He had succeeded in identifying himself, his family, and all his interests with the State and its interests, in a way of which Sulla had never dreamt, and which had not been possible for Julius Caesar. When he restored the Free State he divided the work of government with the Senate and the magistrates, and in this division he took care that the whole range of what we should call imperial and foreign affairs should fall to himself, with the sole command of the army. Thus he became supreme ruler of all provinces on or near the frontiers, appointed their governors, and kept them responsible to himself. If there was war on a frontier, it was carried through by his lieutenants, under his *imperium* and his auspices. For a governor to wage war on his own account was no longer possible, for it was made high treason under a new and stringent law. The safety of the Empire, and especially of the frontier provinces, depended on the army, and the army was now identified once more in interest through Augustus with the State.

But of course a system like this would not work of itself; it needed constant looking after. Augustus knew this well, and knew also that he could not by himself either set it going or continue to look after it.

It was part of his good fortune that he found a really capable and loyal helper in Agrippa, a tried soldier and organizer, who till his death in 12 B.C., during the most prosperous years of Augustus's power, was able to identify his own interests with those of his friend and the State. The two worked admirably together, and between them found time to travel over the whole Empire, working hard at settlements of all kinds, and conducting military operations where they were absolutely necessary. It was the same kind of work, but on a far larger scale, as that of Pompeius after his conquests in the East: founding new cities, and settling the status of old ones: making treaties with kings and chieftains: arranging the details of finance, land-tenure, and so on. Let us notice two important points in all this work of organization, which will help to show how greatly in earnest Augustus was in his task of welding the Empire into real unity, and ruling it on rational principles.

First, he instituted for the first time (though Julius is said to have contemplated it) a complete survey, or *census* as the Romans called it, of all the material resources of the Empire, in order to ascertain what taxes all its free inhabitants ought to pay for purposes of government. Under the Republic there had never been such a survey, and the result was that abundant opportunity had been found for unfair taxation, and for extortion by corrupt officials. Now every house, field and wood was duly valued by responsible officials, so that unjust exactions could be easily detected. By accurate keeping of accounts the government was able to tell what sums it ought to receive, and how much it had to spend; and we know that Augustus's foreign policy was greatly influenced by such financial considerations. He kept a kind of yearly balance-sheet

himself, and his successor found the affairs of the
Empire in perfect order.

Secondly, each province was now for the first time
given a kind of corporate existence, and became something more than the military command of a Roman
magistrate. A council of the province met once a year
at its chief town, and transacted a certain amount of
business. True, this did not give the province any
measure of real self-government, but it had some
useful results, and it is not impossible that Augustus
may have intended that more should eventually follow.
This meeting of a provincial council brought each
province into direct touch with the home government,
and in particular enabled it to make complaint of its
governor if he had been unpopular and oppressive.
And one most interesting feature of these councils was
that they had a worship of their own, meant, no doubt,
to dim the lustre of local and tribal worships, and to
keep the idea of Rome and her rulers constantly before
the minds of the provincials. For the divine objects
of worship were Augustus himself or his Genius, in
combination with the new goddess Roma. The most
famous example of this worship is found at Lugdunum,
now Lyons, where there was an altar dedicated to Rome
and Augustus, at the junction of Rhône and Saône,
which served as a religious centre for the three provinces into which Augustus now divided the great area
of the Gallic conquests of Julius.

Though his object was undoubtedly peace, Augustus
could not, of course, entirely escape war on his frontiers.
He could not have finally settled the frontier on the line
of the Danube, which was far the most valuable military
work of his time, without wars which were both long
and dangerous. It was absolutely necessary to cover
Italy on the north-east, where the passes over the Alps

are low and comparatively easy, and also to shield the Greek peninsula from attack by the wild tribes to the north of it. I have already alluded to the great work of Tiberius (the stepson of Augustus) in this quarter, which marks him as the third of the great generals who saved the civilization of the Mediterranean for us. At one time Augustus thought of advancing the frontier from the Rhine to the Elbe, and so of connecting Elbe and Danube in one continuous line of defence. But this plan made it necessary to enclose all Germany west of the Elbe in the Roman Empire, and it was soon found that the Germans were not to be made into Roman provincials, without a prolonged struggle for which Augustus had neither money nor inclination. So the frontier came back to the Rhine, and the Rhine and the sea marked the Roman frontier on north and west, until Claudius, the third successor of Augustus, added our island, or rather the southern part of it, to the Empire, in A.D. 43.

In the East Augustus contrived to do without war, trusting, and rightly trusting, to the enormous prestige he had won by overcoming Antony and Cleopatra, and annexing the ancient kingdom of Egypt. His fame spread to India, and probably even to China, with the caravans of merchants who then as now passed along fixed routes from Syria and Egypt to the Far East. We Britons know what *prestige* can do among Orientals; it is a word that has often been in disfavour, but it means that there are ways of avoiding war without withdrawing just claims to influence. Augustus contrived on the strength of his prestige to keep an honourable peace with the Parthians and Armenians who bordered on the Empire along the line of the Euphrates, and his successors would have kept it too had they always followed out his policy. Tiberius, his faithful pupil and successor, did follow out that policy, and showed consummate skill in handling it.

The mention of Tiberius, who succeeded to the position of Augustus at the end of his long life, suggests a few words about a weak point in the new system, which was to give some trouble in the future. How was the succession to be effected? Augustus had not made a new constitution; he had only engrafted his own position of authority on the old republican constitution. So at least he wished his position to be understood, and so he was careful to describe it in the record of his deeds which he left behind him, engraved outside the entrance to the great tomb which he built for himself and his family. In dignity and consequence he wished to be considered the first citizen; and this he expressed by the word *Princeps*, i.e. the first man in the State: by the name Augustus, which suggested to a Roman ear something in the nature of religious sanctity: by the honorary title *pater patriae* (father of his country), and in other ways. The real power in his hands had its basis and guarantee in the army, of which his *imperium* made him (as we should say) commander-in-chief; but the army was on the frontiers doing duty for the Empire, all but invisible to the Roman and Italian. Thus his *imperium*, though it might be legally used in Italy, was primarily a military power indispensable for the guardian of the frontiers. To the Italians it might well seem that the Free State was still maintained, and that no new permanent power had been established; though Greeks and foreigners might be, and indeed were, more discerning as to what had really happened.

But when Augustus died, in A.D. 14, how was a succession to be effected? Or was there to be a succession at all—would it not be better to let the State pass back again into the hands of the Senate and people? This last was the only logical way, and it was the plan actually adopted in form. A position like that of Augustus could not pass to a successor, unless the State in its old constitutional form chose to appoint such a successor with the same authority as that of Augustus. To this, however, we must add (and it well shows the real change that had been effected by the long revolution) that no choice of Senate and people could hold good unless the consent of the army could be secured.

Of course Augustus had considered all this, and had made his own plans. He would choose a member of his own family, one, that is, who inherited the name and fame of Caesar by blood or adoption, would adopt him as a son (for he had no son of his own), make him his heir, associate him as far as possible in his own dignity and authority, and thus mark him out as the natural heir to the principate. This would make it difficult for Senate or army to refuse him; beyond that Augustus knew that he could not go. He was unlucky in losing one after another the youths whom he thus destined to succeed him, and eventually had to fall back on his stepson Tiberius: a great soldier, as we have seen, and a man of integrity and ability, but of reserved and even morose temper, and one with whom the shrewd and genial Augustus had little in common.

When Augustus died there was an anxious moment. There was no reason why the principate should be confined to the family of the Caesars, nor any reason but expediency for having a *princeps* at all. But, after all, the will of the dead ruler prevailed, and Tiberius slipped into his place without opposition; the Senate accepted him as plainly marked out by Augustus, and the army raised no difficulty, though his nephew

Germanicus Caesar was young, popular, and in actual command of the army on the Rhine. Some mocking voices were heard, and throughout his principate of twenty-three years Tiberius had to endure continual annoyance from the old republican families, but there was no real attempt to quarrel with the principate as an institution of the Roman State.

I have dwelt on this point at some length in order to show what a singular creation this principate of Augustus was. To proclaim monarchy outright would probably have been fatal; to take the whole work on himself would be to leave the old governing families idle and discontented; on the other hand, to do the necessary work as a yearly elected magistrate, according to the old practice, was plainly impossible. Election by the people of the Roman city would have little force in the eyes of the Empire, and it was this Empire as a whole that Augustus wished to represent. The course he took shows him a shrewd, observant, tactical diplomatist, if ever there was one. He is not a man on whose character we dwell with sympathy or enthusiasm; he does not kindle our admiration like C. Gracchus or Caesar; but he was essentially the man for the hour.

To him we owe in large measure the glories of 'the Augustan age', with its poets, historians, and artists; it was the 'Augustan peace', and the encouragement and patronage of Augustus, that enabled Horace to write his perfect lyrics and his good-natured comments on human life, Ovid to pour forth his abundant stream of beautiful versification, Tibullus and Propertius to sing of the Italian country and its deities and festivals, and Livy, the greatest of Roman historians, to do in noble prose what Virgil had done in noble verse—to inspire Romans and Italians with enthusiasm for the great deeds of their ancestors. But the world owes Augustus a still greater debt than this; for he laid securely the foundations of an imperial system strong enough to save for us, through centuries of danger, the priceless treasures of Graeco-Roman civilization.

K

CHAPTER IX

LIFE IN THE ROMAN EMPIRE

Now that we have seen the Empire made comparatively secure by Augustus, and set in the way of development on what seem to be rational principles, let us pause and try to gain some idea of the social life going on within it: excluding that of the city of Rome, which is no longer of the old paramount importance. How did the inhabitants of the Empire live and occupy themselves during the first two centuries of our era?

The first point to make quite clear is that this life was in the main a life in towns. Roman policy had always favoured the maintenance of existing towns, except in the very rare cases where they were deemed too dangerous. Carthage and Corinth had been destroyed by Rome on this pretext, but they had been founded afresh by Julius Caesar, and were now beginning a long and vigorous city life. In the East, where city-states abounded, Rome retained and adorned them, or built new ones, as Pompey did after crushing Mithradates and Tigranes. In the West, in Gaul and Spain, where they did not exist at all, she founded some, and by a wonderfully wise policy favoured the natural growth of others. The people of these western provinces lived chiefly in some kind of villages, scattered over a district which we may call a canton, often, perhaps, as big as an English county of to-day. The Roman policy was either to found a city to serve as the centre of the canton, and to endow it with magistrates and senate on the Roman model:

or to give the canton its senate and magistrates, and leave it to develop its own town-centre.

This policy shows extremely well the genius of Rome for civilizing or Romanizing, without destroying the grouping and the habits of the people to be civilized, or Romanized. The old tribal (or cantonal) system remained, and its officers were the chiefs of the old population; but they now bore Roman names, *duoviri*, *quaestores*, and so on, and sat in an assembly called *ordo* —i.e. senate. If a town were not founded at once, in which the business of the canton could be carried on, it was certain to grow of itself. A purely rural region, where the people live in villages only, was contrary to Roman interests and traditions; it was inconvenient for raising taxes, and it did not give those opportunities of culture and amusement which the Roman looked for when he travelled or settled in a province. The provincials, too, were in this way made more happy and contented; town life greatly helped in civilizing them, attracting the better or richer people from the villages.

To help us in realizing this urban character of Roman provincial life, we may compare it with that of the population of India at the present day. India is still in the main a rural country, and by far the great majority of its inhabitants live on the land and support themselves by agriculture. The economic unit of India is the village, and this simple fact is enough to explain why India never has been Anglicized. Instinctively the Romans perceived that if a province were to be Romanized, the process could not be set going in villages; and where there were only villages, they gave the districts the opportunity of developing towns in their midst. The opportunity, we may reasonably suppose, was rarely missed, for at all times in their history the Romans had a wonderful power of making their subjects eager to imitate their own institutions. Thus Spain, Gaul, and even Britain became rich in towns after the Roman model—towns which served to humanize the people, while making them obedient subjects.

Let us now see, with the help of a few striking examples, how, by the second century of our era, the Empire was covered with towns. For Italy and Greece we do not need illustrations—we are already well aware of the fact. But even far away in the East, in regions where the Greeks had never settled, if the Romans came to stay they left cities behind them. Look, for example, at a map of Syria or Palestine, and note the great caravan route leading from Damascus southwards on the east side of the Jordan, a road important to Rome because it carried the merchandise of the Far East to Damascus and the Mediterranean by way of the Persian Gulf and Petra. Before the traveller of to-day has gone far south from Damascus he will come on the splendid ruins of two successive cities built by the Romans in this period, Gerasa and Philadelphia, where the sheep now graze among the ruins of temples, theatres, and baths. A famous English traveller [1] wrote of them long ago that they enabled him to form some conception of the grandeur and might of the Roman Empire: 'That cities so far removed from the capital, and built almost in the desert, should have been adorned with so many splendid monuments, afforded one of the most striking proofs of the marvellous energy and splendid enterprise of that great people who had subjected the world.'

The mention of Damascus may remind us of a traveller of the first century A.D. whose journeys are fortunately recorded and admirably illustrate the fact

[1] Sir A. H Layard.

that in Asia Minor and Greece the life of the people was centred in the great cities. St. Paul went from city to city, choosing by preference for his missionary work the most populous ones, such as Antioch, Ephesus, Thessalonica, Corinth and Athens.

Passing westwards, and leaving out of account the many cities of Egypt, we shall find that what has been so far said holds good of the Roman province of Africa. This province eventually became one of the most highly cultured as well as populous, mainly owing to its numerous towns. Of many of these the remains still astonish the traveller. A photograph lies before me of one of them which still stands almost in the desert, silent and abandoned, with temples, streets, and all the belongings of a great city as perfect as at the excavated Pompeii, which was overwhelmed in A.D. 79 by the great eruption of Vesuvius. An inscription tells us that Thamugadi was founded in A.D. 100, and built with the help of a legion of Roman soldiers to guard civilization against the marauders of the desert. Another of these towns is a good example of the way in which the army contributed to the policy of creating town-centres; Lambaesis, the modern Lambèse, at the foot of the Djebel-Aurès in Algeria, was the permanent station of a military force, round which there grew up a civil population of traders and camp-followers. Great roads, here as everywhere in the Empire, connected these towns with each other and with the capital of the province, in this case Carthage.

If we cross the sea from Africa to Gaul or Spain we shall find the same process going on. Spain we must pass by; but in Gaul we land at the ancient Greek city of Massilia, which, as Marseilles, is still the great port of southern France. A little to the north, Nîmes (Nemausus) was formed into a city by Augustus out of a rural population; its vast Roman amphitheatre and an exquisitely beautiful temple belong to the second century, and still stand in the middle of the modern city. Lyons also was founded by Augustus, as we saw in the last chapter, with a special purpose. Farther north the cities on the great roads were gradually formed, out of tribal populations living in villages, and many of them still bear the names of those tribes: Paris is the town-centre of the Parisii, Rheims of the Remi, Soissons of the Suessiones, Trier of the Treveri. This last city, on the Moselle, can boast of more imposing Roman work than any north of Italy, and is within comparatively easy reach of visitors from our shores.

Britain, which was invaded and made a province in the reign of Claudius, was never so fully Romanized as other provinces, partly owing to the wild and stubborn nature of its inhabitants; but even in our midst the Roman has left obvious traces of his belief in town life. London's origin as a trading-centre may just, perhaps, antedate the coming of the Romans, but its rapid growth and expansion certainly owed much to them. Apart from London, however, nearly all the first Roman towns had a more directly military origin and object. The oldest of them is Colchester, a military colony, which still has its Roman walls. Then came St. Albans (Verulamium), Gloucester, Chester, Lincoln and York, strategical points of importance, where populous cities still stand. Some of these towns have disappeared, and have been recovered only by excavation, e.g. Calleva (Silchester, near Basingstoke), the town-centre of the Atrebates; but many of our country towns, besides those just mentioned, still stand on ancient Roman sites, and even without much excavation have yielded traces of their Roman inhabitants. At such places as Dorchester, Silchester, and Caerleon-on-Usk we can still see the remains of an amphitheatre; while St. Albans, and even such a small community as Brough-on-Humber (near Hull) could boast of a theatre. All our towns and villages of which the names contain the word *chester* or *cester* are Roman in origin, though they may not have been large cities like Gloucester (Glevum); for *chester* is only our English form of *castra*, the Latin for a military encampment.

If it is now quite clear that the town is the unit of civilization in the Empire, what was the social and political life of the town? Of this we know now much more than we used to do, for it is mirrored in the many thousands of inscriptions from every Roman province, which through many years were collected and correctly published under the direction of the famous Theodor Mommsen, whose name cannot be omitted entirely, even in such an unpretending book about Rome as this. In records on stone there is, indeed, something lacking that can only be supplied by literature, which reports more elaborately and earnestly the thoughts and feelings of men; and in the Empire, apart from Italy and Rome, there is but little literature to help us out. But the inscriptions supply us with the necessary facts.

First, of the political condition of these innumerable towns we may say that it shows diversity in unity. There were several grades of privilege among them. Some were nominally independent of the Roman government, and in alliance with it, but these were few; Athens is the most famous example. Others were communities of Roman citizens; and many had the Latin right, i.e. inferior privilege. Lastly, there were great numbers of cities—a majority of the whole number—whose inhabitants were not Roman citizens at all, but directly under the control of the governor of their province, who was limited in his authority over the more privileged and independent towns. So much for diversity.

But all the cities were in reality governed and organized in much the same way. In each there was a constitution closely resembling that of Rome, and in most instances modelled directly upon it. As at Rome, they had yearly elected magistrates, who, after holding office, passed into a senate of advisers and councillors; and these magistrates were elected by the *populus*, or the whole body of citizens. Here was plenty of useful work to do, as we can guess from our own experience of local self-government. Plutarch, writing in this period of his own little town of Chaeronea in Greece, realizes this to the full, and urges that the work of the magistrate is honourable work, and the more so as it is combined with the sense of citizenship in a great empire.

There was, however, a tendency in these provincial towns, as in the city of Rome itself, for the magistrate, who must be a man of substance, to undertake the expense of amusing the people; a tendency to make the people dependent on the rich for their comforts rather than on their own industry and exertion. The magistrate, besides paying a large fee on his accession to office, was expected to give public games, to feast the people, or to give them a present of money all round. And he would wish, too, to distinguish his magistracy by erecting some public buildings—a bath, aqueduct, or theatre; or to endow a school. So it came to pass in course of time that his burdens were heavier than he could bear, and that the whole class to which he belonged, the senatorial one, was involved in the same difficulties. This class could not be recruited from the common people, who rarely had the means, or, indeed, the energy, to rise to affluence; and the tendency as time went on was to draw the line ever more sharply between the dignity of the various classes. But the ruin of the senatorial class, or *curiales*, lies outside our limits.

The lower class was engaged in industry, either on the land, or in the town itself. This industry was not to any large extent employed by capital, nor was it in competition with slave-labour, of which in provincial towns we do not hear much. The members of the various trades and callings worked on their own account, but were almost invariably grouped together in gilds or associations, and these are one of the most interesting features in the life of this period. Each of these gilds was licensed, or should have been licensed, by the central government at Rome—a good example of the way in which the long arm of that government reached to every provincial town through the agency of the provincial governor and his officials. Illegal association was a serious crime, and this was one of the reasons why the small Christian communities were looked on with suspicion by the government.

What was the object of these associations? The question has often been asked whether they were in any sense provident societies like our friendly societies, and, on the whole, the conclusion of investigators has been that they were not. If we had more literature dealing with provincial life, or such a correspondence as that of Cicero and his friends, we could give a more certain answer.

But in one sense at least they may be called provident societies. All, or nearly all, of them had as one main object the assurance of a proper tomb and decent

funeral for the members. This object can be fully
appreciated only after some real study of the social life
and religion of that and the preceding age, but when it
is understood it is inexpressibly touching. It would
seem that the life of the working man of that day was
by no means an unhappy one, that he was not driven
or enslaved by an employer, nor forced to live in
grimy and unwholesome surroundings. So far as we
can tell he had little anxiety in this life, and worshipped
his gods, and performed his vows to them, with genuine
gratitude. But that he should be utterly neglected
and forgotten after death, thrown into some common
grave to moulder away unnoticed, 'where no hand
would bring the annual offering of wine and flowers'—
this seems to have been the shadow ever hanging over
his life. We may doubt whether the hope of immor-
tality had, as a rule, anything to do with this anxiety.
It was rather an inherited instinct than a faith or creed
that moved these poor people. Originally it had been
the desire not to have to wander as a ghost for lack of
due burial; now it is rather the fear that they might
be forgotten by those left behind, or, indeed, by future
generations.

The instinct of association is common to man, and
in a vast empire, where the tendency was, and long
had been, to obliterate the old social grouping of
kinship, real or supposed, it would be some consolation
to belong to a club of friends with common interests,
accustomed to share the joys and perils of life, and bent
on decent burial when death should overtake them.
Even in this life they would meet from time to time
to eat, drink and enjoy themselves.

On the whole, we may conclude that this life of the
towns was a happy one, so long as the frontiers were
well guarded and no sudden raid or invasion by an

enemy was likely; so long, too, as person and property were securely protected under Roman law administered without corruption, and amusements and conveniences were to be had for little or nothing. But undoubtedly something was wanting; there was mischief in the social system somewhere, though it was not easy to lay finger upon it. The sap was running in the plant too feebly; there was a lack of keen industrial energy and of the instinct of self-help. As time went on, the central government grew too paternal, interfered too much in the life of these towns, and so encouraged the tendency to 'slackness'. And more and more, as pressure came on the Empire from without, the play of life in these once happy cities became an automatic movement of machinery, the central wheel of which was the Caesar at Rome.

Another aspect of the life of the provincial towns must be mentioned here, which suggests that the trend of the time was not entirely healthy. I said at the beginning of this book that the great monuments left behind her by Rome were mainly of a useful and practical kind, e.g. roads, aqueducts, places of business. This is true, but it is now necessary to add that some of the most imposing of these fabrics were, in the period we have now reached, entirely devoted to amusement, and amusement of a kind neither educative nor humane. The taste had long been growing at Rome for spectacles of bloodshed—combats of gladiators, and the hunting of wild beasts in a confined space; and from Rome this degraded taste passed only too rapidly into the provinces. Most large provincial towns had their amphitheatre, in imitation of the huge one at Rome, which we know as the Colosseum; and the more fully Romanized a province was, the more of these homes of inhumanity were to be found in it. The most magnificent one still standing outside Italy, that at Nîmes, dates, strange to say, from the mild and enlightened age of the Antonines, to which we are coming in the next chapter. The Greeks, indeed, generally took less interest in such shows; but in the western provinces, where the best and most virile populations of the Empire were now to be found, their effect was beyond doubt pernicious, for they encouraged not only inhumanity, but idleness. Day after day the greater part of the population of a city might sit and watch lazily these bloody entertainments, on which, perhaps, some wealthy citizen was wasting his capital to his own ruin.

As may, perhaps, be said of ourselves in this present age, the Romans of the Empire were being encouraged to live too much in the enjoyment of the present, without anxiety for the future. So, too, the cultured classes gradually came to look back at the past, to the great achievements of Rome in war and literature, as all in all to them, and lost the desire to strike out new lines, to make new discoveries, to try new experiments. 'Over all, to our eyes, there broods the shadow which haunts the life that is nourished only by memories, and to which the future sends no call and offers no promise.'[1]

[1] Dill, *Roman Society in the Last Century of the Western Empire*, 2nd ed., 1899, p. 194.

CHAPTER X

THE EMPIRE UNDER THE ANTONINES
CONCLUSION

THE chief work of Rome in the world, as has often been said in this little book, was the defence of Mediterranean civilization against external enemies. That work was of a double nature. It could not be done simply by marking out and holding lines of frontier; it was also necessary so to organize the Empire within its frontiers that the whole should contribute to the common object, with men, money and public spirit. The last two chapters will have shown that from the time of Julius and Augustus Roman rulers fully recognized this twofold nature of their task. Augustus in particular, while gradually settling the frontiers on a system well thought out, and adapted to his means and experience, also spent much time and pains on internal organization. He found the Empire a loose collection of subject territories, each governed, well or ill as it might happen, by an officer almost independent of the central authority; he left it, at the end of his long life, in the way of becoming a well-compacted whole, in which every part felt more or less the force of a just central government; a civilized State 'standing out in clear relief against the surrounding barbarism'.

In such an empire there must, of course, be differences of race and language—differences, too, of habits, feelings, modes of thought; but under just and wise rule such differences need be no hindrance to the political unity of the whole. There is a book of this period, within the reach of every one, which illustrates better than any other this unity in diversity of the

Roman Empire—I mean the Acts of the Apostles.
It should be studied carefully, with maps and such
other helps as may be available, down to the last
chapter, where it leaves St. Paul at Rome, living in his
own hired house, in the centre of Mediterranean life
and government, teaching undisturbed.

Under the immediate successors of Augustus,
Tiberius, Claudius and Nero, his policy was, on the
whole, maintained with good faith and discretion; and
during the last thirty years of the first century A.D.
Vespasian and his two sons, Titus and Domitian, did
little more than improve the working of the machinery
of his government. More and more, it is true, the
constitution became a real monarchy; the part played
in it by the Senate of the free State was getting steadily
narrowed; but this was all in the interest of efficiency,
and, so far as we can see, it was necessary to the internal
development of the Empire. The Caesars of the first
century must have the credit of ruling wisely, with
the help of their advisers, on the Augustan principles.
True, the great literary genius of the age, the historian
Tacitus, by drawing brilliant and lurid portraits of
some of them, has diverted our attention from their
work as agents of a great system; but to tell their story
as Tacitus has told it is neither possible nor necessary
here. I may pass them over and go on to the second
century and the age of the Antonines, which has rightly
been judged by historians to be the most brilliant and
the happiest in all Roman history.

That four men of what seems to us 'right judgement
in all things' should succeed each other in power at
this critical time is one more example of the wonderful
good fortune of Rome. All were men of capacity and
education, hard workers and conscientious, and they
seem to have communicated their good qualities to

their subordinates, for they never wanted for loyal helpers. The Senate, indeed, was now of little avail for actual work, and the greater part of the business had long been done by Caesar [1] and his own 'servants', freedmen for the most part, often ambitious and unscrupulous Greeks; but in this period, as we shall see directly, the civil service, as we may call it, was placed on a sound and honourable basis. It would seem as if the ideas of duty and discipline were once more to prevail throughout the Roman official world.

The first of the four rulers, Ulpius Traianus, known to us all as Trajan, was not of Roman or even Italian birth, but came from the province of further Spain: a fact which marks the growth of the idea that every part of the Empire may now be turned to account for the common good. Trajan was a soldier by breeding and disposition, and his contribution to the work of this period was mainly a military one. The frontier along the Danube, the last (as we have seen) to be settled, had always been the weakest; and yet here henceforward was to be the most dangerous point in the Empire's line of defence. Along the whole length of the lower Danube a great mass of barbarian tribes was already pressing, pressed themselves from behind by others to north and east. And here, to the north of the river, a great kingdom had been founded by a king of the Dacian people, which corresponds roughly with the modern Rumania. A glance at a map of the Empire will show that such a kingdom would be a standing menace to Italy, to Greece, and even to the peninsula of Asia Minor, and from the Roman point of view Trajan was quite justified in his determination

[1] This is the title by which the *princeps* was usually known in the Empire; see e.g. Matthew xxii. 17 foll., or Acts xxv. 10 foll.

to conquer and annex it. He carried out this policy in two successive wars, with consummate daring and skill. Dacia became a Roman province, and lasted as such long enough (about 170 years) to be an effectual help to imperial defence in this quarter. The story of the two wars is told in the marvellous series of sculptures forming a spiral round the Column of Trajan, which stood and still stands at Rome in the forum built by him and called by his name.

Towards the end of his life Trajan embarked on a new policy in the East, and failed to carry it out. The shrewd Augustus, as we saw, had trusted here to his prestige, knowing that war in this region was both perilous and expensive. Since then both peril and expense had been incurred here under Nero, but his policy produced fifty years of peace. Trajan, however, provoked by a move of the Parthian king, made up his mind to seize Armenia, the old bone of contention between Rome and Parthia, and not only did this, but added by conquest two other provinces, Mesopotamia and Assyria. Some historians have thought his judgement as good here as it was on the Danube. The best way of deciding the question is to look carefully at a map of the Empire and then to ask oneself whether these territories were really needed for the protection of Mediterranean civilization. For myself I unhesitatingly answer in the negative; but there is no need to dispute the point here, as Trajan died before he had made his conquests secure. The Jews, dispersed all over these regions, urged by their implacable hatred of Rome, stirred up rebellion in Trajan's rear with alarming ferocity, and in the middle of this turmoil he died on his way back to Rome. His successor Hadrian at once renounced any attempt to keep the new provinces.

It would be unjust to the memory of a great man if we were to think of Trajan as a soldier only. He was a strenuous man, unsparing of himself in any part of his duty. He pursued a policy of public benefit in Italy, striving, like Augustus, to encourage agriculture and population, and carrying out a plan of his predecessor Nerva for providing a fund for the education of poor children. This last institution became an important one, and shows well how really benevolent—perhaps even to excess—how anxious for the well-being of Italy, were the Caesars of the second century. Money was lent by the State to the Italian farmers in need of it, and the interest, at five per cent., was appropriated to the education of boys up to eighteen and girls up to fourteen years of age.

Trajan bestowed the same minute care on the provinces. In most of these there was no trouble, but in one case, Bithynia, which had been under Senatorial governors, he had to send out a special commissioner to repair neglect and mischief. Luckily for us it happened that this commissioner was Pliny the younger, nephew of the great encyclopaedist of the same name; and Pliny was so prominent a figure of the time that his correspondence has been preserved. That part of it which contains his letters to Trajan, and Trajan's brief and pithy answers, is one of the most precious treasures that have survived from ancient literature. Pliny consults him on a variety of details, some of them almost ludicrously petty, some of them of general importance, such as a famous one about his policy towards the Christians; and the answers show us Trajan as a shrewd and sensible man, fully aware that in such a unity as the Roman Empire there must needs be diversity, and that governors must learn to adapt themselves to such diversity without

losing hold of the principles of justice and equity.
Before we leave this subject it may be as well to mention
that this constant interchange of letters between
persons more than a thousand miles apart need astonish
no one. In the interest of imperialism the public posts
had been thoroughly organized by Augustus; the
roads were excellent, the shipping well seen to, and
travelling was at least as easy and rapid as it was in
England till the beginning of the Railway Age.

Trajan's strong and rather rugged features, familiar
to all students of the Empire, are in striking contrast
to those of his three successors. He was clean-shaven,
but his next successor, Hadrian, introduced the
practice of wearing his beard, and this was adhered to.
All the imperial portraits of this age, as preserved on
coins and sculptures, are perfectly authentic, and the
likenesses are consistent. In the British Museum the
reader may see the features of these great Caesars as
faithfully reproduced as those of British statesmen in
the National Portrait Gallery.

Trajan was succeeded by his cousin Hadrian,
beyond doubt one of the most capable and efficient
men who ever wielded great power. No one can study
his reign without feeling that it was better in this age,
if an efficient man could be found, that his hand alone
should be on the helm. Probably Hadrian was only
one of many who might have done as well as he did,
for there was now a spirit abroad of intelligent industry
directed to the good of the State; yet it is almost certain
that the Empire was the better for not having the
sovereignty put into commission. It has been well
said of Hadrian that he desired 'to see himself all
that was to be seen, to know all that was to be known,
to do all that was to be done'; and subsequent events
proved that this intelligent industry could hardly have

been carried all through the imperial work with equal effect had it been shared with others.

Hadrian accomplished his work by two long periods of travel, each lasting over four years. Without any pomp or state he made himself acquainted with all parts of the Empire and their needs, as no ruler had done since Augustus and Agrippa shared such a task between them. The more immediate object was to inspect the frontiers and secure them, and as Hadrian was a trained soldier, with much experience under Trajan, this was to him familiar work. But he was so full of curiosity, so anxious to see all that the Empire had to show him, that while he practised his indefatigable industry he could also gratify his intelligence. In this he was more like Julius Caesar than any other Roman we know of, though in most traits of character he was very different from that great man. It is not possible here to describe Hadrian's frontier work in detail, but a specimen of it shall be given which should be interesting to British readers.

Britain had been invaded by the emperor Claudius in the year 43, and the southern part of the island had been made into a Roman province. Since then the frontier had been pushed farther north, and the legionary garrisons were no longer Colchester and Gloucester, but Caerleon, Chester and York. Hadrian spent several months here in the course of his first journey, and his visit had a remarkable result which we can see with our eyes at this moment. He must have noted two facts: first, the unsettled and rebellious condition of the natives of Yorkshire and Northumberland (Brigantes): and secondly, the narrow waist of the island between the Solway Firth and the mouth of the Tyne. He must have reasoned that if Roman forces could be permanently established on a fortified line between the two seas, this line would serve as a check on the Brigantes, and also as a base of operations for further advance northwards.

Thus it is that 'Hadrian's Wall' remains as the most striking of all Roman works in our island. We know that the emperor, coming from the Rhine in 122, brought one of his best commanders, Platorius Nepos, with him to carry it out: a stone wall, just over 73 miles long, was constructed from what is still called Wallsend (east of Newcastle) to Carlisle, and beyond to Bowness-on-Solway. When completed it must have stood some twenty feet high, with a deep ditch in front, and behind it a road running along its whole length; a little to the south, a great earthwork, the so-called *vallum*—a ditch twenty-five feet wide—was dug possibly to prevent undesirable or disloyal natives from entering the military zone. Large fortified stations were set at intervals along the wall, and at about every Roman mile there were fortified passages through it, now called 'milecastles', seventy-nine in all. The country north of the Wall was occupied, forts built and roads laid down in Scottish territory, and in 142 the Roman governor of Britain erected another wall, this time in turf, between the Forth and the Clyde. From this date till 211 the Scottish lowlands counted as a part of the Empire. But though the conquest of the Highlands was never carried through permanently, and though after 211 the northern frontier followed roughly the present boundary-line between England and Scotland, Hadrian's great work had an immense moral effect on the population to the south of it, and Britain became very substantially Romanized. Towns and country houses (*villae*) sprang up in abundance along or near the military roads. As I write these lines in North Oxfordshire, I have the remains of several of these *villae* within easy reach, and can visit, each in a day, at least four considerable Roman towns—Cirencester, Gloucester, Silchester (Calleva), and last, but not least, Bath (Aquae Sulis), where the Romans found and used, as they always did in such spots, the magnificent hot springs, building noble baths about them which may be seen to this day.

Hadrian's care for the good working of the civil government was as great as his zeal for frontier defence. Two forward steps were taken by him in this department, both of which helped on that consolidation of the Empire which was his constant aim.

First, he organized and dignified the civil service, on which the actual good working of the whole system depended. Caesar's share in this work had steadily been increasing while that of the Senate diminished; yet Caesar had so far done his part, as we saw just now, with the help only of his own personal 'servants', who were mostly freedmen, i.e. slaves by origin, and many of them Greeks. Hadrian now established a public imperial civil service, of which the members must be Roman knights, i.e. men of a certain consequence in regard to birth and property. These new civil servants were excused all military service, and could thus be trained to the work without interruption, during their earlier years.

Secondly, we may date from Hadrian's reign the beginning of the consolidation of Roman law, and the rise of a school of great lawyers such as the world has never known since. Apart from the defence of Mediterranean civilization, to which, indeed, its indirect contribution was not small, this was the most valuable legacy of Rome to modern Europe. Law had originally consisted mainly of the old legal rules of the city-state of Rome, embodied in the Twelve Tables, and a few

statutes; but, in course of time, through the need of
interpreting these, and adjusting them to the customs
of other peoples in the Empire, an immense body of
what we may call *judgement law* had arisen in the form
of edicts or public notices of magistrates, issued both
in Italy and the provinces. As these customs were
now well known, and as the Empire had reached its
limits, it was possible to close and consolidate this
huge body of official decisions and precedents; and
this was done under Hadrian's direction. The other
two sources of law were still to grow largely before
they could be welded into the great 'Body of
Law' (*Corpus Juris*) compiled under the orders of
Justinian in the sixth century, which is still the
chief European textbook of legal studies. These two
sources were the delivered opinions of wise
lawyers on points of law, and the decisions of the
Caesars in various forms, all of which had the force
of law.

The death of Hadrian in A.D. 138 brings us to the
third of the great Caesars of this age, Titus Antoninus, a
man who, at fifty-two, had already done excellent work
for the Empire. He is known to history as Antoninus
Pius, and this last name, given him apparently on his
accession, may be a reminiscence of Virgil's epithet
for his hero, and may be due to the strong sense of
duty which marked his whole life, public and private.
He seems, indeed, vividly to recall the ideal of the
Roman character as we traced it in the third chapter
of this book; yet he was not Italian by birth. His
family belonged to Nîmes in southern Gaul, and that
ancient city still honours him with a 'Place Antonin',
in which his statue stands. His features, as they appear
on portrait busts, entirely confirm the account of him
left us by his nephew and successor. Grave and wise,

gentle yet firm, religious in the true old Roman sense, pure in life, and simple in all his needs and pleasures, he ruled over a peaceful and contented empire, devoting himself to the work of humanizing and softening the life and lot of his subjects.

Let us glance, for example, at his attitude towards slavery, which, when we last noticed it, was threatening to become a deadly poison in the Roman system. During the first century of the Empire, chiefly under the influence of the Stoic philosophy, as later on under that of Christianity, there had been growing up a feeling that a slave was, after all, a human being, and had some claim to be treated as such under the Roman law, beneficent in its dealings with all other human beings. Antoninus followed out this new idea both in legislation and in his private life, as did his successor also, who adored his memory. They limited the right of a master over his slaves in several ways; ordaining that if cruelty were proved against a master, he should be compelled to sell the slave he had ill-treated. It is noteworthy, too, that the philosopher in whom they most delighted, Epictetus, had himself originally been a slave. There is no better way of realizing the spirit of humanity which actuated Antoninus and his successor than by making some acquaintance with the moral philosophy of Epictetus, and the *Meditations* of Marcus Aurelius.

Hadrian had left the Empire well guarded, and it does not seem to have occurred to Antoninus to see for himself that Hadrian's vigilance was maintained. This was the one weak point of his reign, and it cost his successors dear. He stayed in Italy, concerned as little as possible with wars or rumours of wars; he lived tranquilly, and died peacefully, without trouble or anxiety. But we know that even before his death clouds were beginning to gather on the northern frontier; and we cannot but feel that the beautiful tranquillity of Antoninus's life was hardly compatible with the duty of an imperial guardian.

Marcus Aurelius, the author of the *Meditations*, succeeded his uncle and adoptive father in A.D. 161. Though not the greatest of the four as a ruler, he was the most remarkable as a man, and holds a higher place than the others in the world's esteem. We may find parallels in history to Trajan, less easily, perhaps, to Hadrian and Antoninus; but there is no monarch like Marcus Aurelius, not even in the history of the Jews. It is, indeed, astonishing that Rome, Rome of the hard practical temperament, should have produced a ruler who was a philosopher and almost a saint, and yet capable of government. It is the last striking manifestation of the old Roman spirit of duty and discipline, now kindled into a real ethical emotion by the teaching of the Stoics, far the most inspiring creed then available for a man of action. Without any aid from Christianity, which, indeed, he could not understand and occasionally persecuted, Marcus learnt not only how to make his own life pure, but how to live and work for the world of his day.

But saintliness on the throne, as in the case of St. Louis of France, has its drawbacks in practical work. It is, perhaps, true that the mind of Marcus was more active, and found greater satisfaction, in questioning itself than in anxious inquiry into the state of the Empire. He was not one of those of whom our poet says that they do Duty's work *and know it not*; and as a consequence his days were not serene and bright. He had a tendency to be morbid, and, like all morbid men, he was serious even to sadness. It has been well said of him that he is always insisting on his faith in a universe in which, nevertheless, he can find nothing but disappointment.

Sensitiveness about duty sometimes warped his judgement and blunted his discernment of character. At the outset he made a bad blunder in dividing the imperial power with his brother by adoption, Lucius Verus, who had little principle and much leaning to pleasure. To him he committed the charge of a war with Parthia which became inevitable, and though the Roman arms were successful, this was not due to the skill or energy of either Marcus or Verus. Had a strong scientific mind been in command, it might have been possible to avert or mitigate a calamity which now fell on the Mediterranean world, and had a share, perhaps a large one, in the decay and fall of the Empire. The legions brought back with them from the East one of the most terrible plagues known to history, which can only be compared for its effects with the Black Death in the fourteenth century.

Not only in the East, but nearer home, Marcus had to meet formidable foes who broke through the frontiers with which Hadrian had taken such pains. Pushed forward by pressure from the rear, German tribes unwillingly made their way into Roman territory, overran the new province of Dacia, crossed the Danube, and even passed over the Alps into Italy. Marcus's difficulties were great, but he met them with patience and courage. The pestilence had so greatly thinned the population that both men and money were wanting for the war, and the struggle to drive back the unwilling invaders was prolonged for thirteen years. It was still going on when Marcus died of fever in camp at Vienna in A.D. 180. As he closed his eyes in his tent he must have felt that he had spent himself in vain, and that evil days were in store for the Empire.

He left a worthless son, Commodus, who failed to understand the danger, and let things slide.

We need not follow the Empire in its downward course. We have seen what the work of Rome in the world was to be, and how at last she accomplished it in spite of constant peril and frequent disaster. From Marcus Aurelius onwards the strain of self-defence was too great to allow of progress in any social or political sense. The monarchy became more absolute, the machinery of government more complicated; the masses were overtaxed, and the middle classes ruined. Depopulation again set in, and attempts to remedy it by settling barbarian invaders within the frontiers had some bad results. Hardly more than a hundred years after Marcus's death the government of the Empire had to be shared between two rulers, one in the East and the other in the West: though Constantine restored the unity of the Empire and in 325 transformed the old Greek town of Byzantium into a great imperial capital (to be called Constantinople, after him), these arrangements could not permanently halt the invaders; at the last they broke through all barriers, and Rome fell.

Yet this did not happen before the name and fame of Rome had made such deep impression on their minds that they sought to deserve the inheritance which had thus fallen to them; despising, indeed, the degenerate provincials who struck no blow in their own defence, but full of respect for the majestic power which had for so many centuries confronted and instructed them.[1] They never swept away the civilization of the Mediterranean; from Julius onwards the Roman rulers had done so much to defend it, had raised its prestige so high, had so thoroughly organized its internal life,

[1] Bryce, *Holy Roman Empire*.

that uncivilized peoples neither could nor would destroy it.

We still enjoy its best fruits—the art, science and literature of Hellas, the genius of Rome for law—for 'the just interference of the State in the interests and passions of humanity'. [1] We may be apt at the present day, when science has opened out for us so many new paths of knowledge, and inspired us with such enthusiasm in pursuing them, to forget the value of the inheritance which Rome preserved for us. But this is merely a passing phase of feeling; it is really quite inconsistent with the character of an age which recognizes the doctrine of evolution as its great discovery. It is natural for civilized man to go back upon his past, and to be grateful for all profit he can gain from the study of his own development. So we may be certain that the claim of Greece and Rome to our eternal gratitude will never cease to be asserted, and their right to teach us still what we could have learnt nowhere else, will never be successfully disputed.

[1] This is Mommsen's definition of Law.

BIBLIOGRAPHY

The following books are suggested as among those likely to be useful to students who wish to pursue the subject further:

1. *Large Histories*

The Cambridge Ancient History, volumes vii to xii, gives a full and comprehensive treatment. Besides this we would name MOMMSEN, *History of Rome to the Death of Caesar* (of which there is a handy reprint in the Everyman Library) and *The Provinces of the Roman Empire*: GIBBON, *The Decline and Fall of the Roman Empire* (edited by J. B. Bury): HEITLAND, *The Roman Republic*: ROSTOVTSEFF, *The Social and Economic History of the Roman Empire*.

2. *Smaller Histories in one Volume*

M. CARY, *History of Rome down to the Reign of Constantine*: T. FRANK, *A History of Rome*: H. STUART JONES, *The Roman Empire*: H. F. PELHAM, *Outlines of Roman History*.

There are many school histories, but these are rather fuller and more interesting.

3. *Books on special Topics*

F. E. ADCOCK, *The Roman Art of War*: J. BUCHAN, *Augustus*: M. P. CHARLESWORTH, *Trade-Routes and Commerce of the Roman Empire*: (Sir) S. DILL, *Roman Society from Nero to Marcus Aurelius*: A. H. J. GREENIDGE, *Roman Public Life*: H. GROSE HODGE, *Roman Panorama*: H. J. HASKELL, *This was Cicero*: W. E. HEITLAND, *Agricola* (A Study of Agriculture and Rustic Life in the Greco-Roman World from the point of view of Labour): A. D. NOCK, *Conversion* (The Old and the New in Religion from Alexander the Great to Augustine of Hippo): H. M. D. PARKER, *The Roman Legions*: C. A. J. SKEEL, *Travel in the First Century after Christ*: R. SYME, *The Roman Revolution*. Among the numerous books of W. WARDE FOWLER should be mentioned especially: *Social Life at Rome in the Age of Cicero*: *The Religious Experience of the Roman People*, and *Roman Essays and Interpretations*.

4. *The Romans in Britain*

R. G. COLLINGWOOD, *Roman Britain*: *The Handbook to the Roman Wall*, 1933 (this being a revision of *The Handbook* by the late J. Collingwood Bruce): F. HAVERFIELD, *The Romanization of Roman Britain*, 3rd edition, 1915: *The Roman Occupation of Britain* (revised by G. Macdonald), 1924. Those who wish to know more about camps or remains or roads in their own region should consult the volumes of the *Victoria County Histories*, or the accounts in the transactions of antiquarian societies such as *Archaeologia Aeliana* or the *Transactions* of the Cumberland and Westmorland Antiquarian Society.

5. *Ancient Authorities in Translation*

Nearly all the works of the great Roman writers—Caesar, Cicero, Horace, Livy, Lucretius, Marcus Aurelius, Ovid, Tacitus and Virgil—can now be read in translations in the Loeb series. Plutarch's *Lives* are published in the Everyman series; the most valuable are those of Cato the Elder, Aemilius Paullus, the two Gracchi, Marius, Sulla, Pompey, Caesar, Cicero, Brutus, and Antony.

INDEX

Actium, battle of, 122
Aeneid, the, 125–7
Agrippa, M. Vipsanius, 131, 155
Alps, the, 65, 96, 97, 111
Antoninus Pius, Emperor, 158–60
Antony, Mark (Marcus Antonius), 122, 128, 133
Apennines, the, 15, 65
Armenia, 107, 152
Army, the Roman, 47 ff., 98, 134, 141
Augustus Caesar, 11, 89, 98, 122, 124 ff., 137–8, 141, 149, 150–5
Auspices, 44

Brindisi, 15, 33, 114
Britain, 142, 143, 155 ff.
Byzantium, 162

Caesar. *See* Augustus; Julius
Campania, 15, 28, 33, 67, 68
Cannae, battle of, 67–9
Carthage, 56–72, 138, 141
Cato the Elder, 10–13, 41, 42, 82
   the Younger, 113
Catullus, 106, 117–19
Caudine Forks, 30
Censors, 53, 54
Census under Empire, 131
Christianity, 130, 145, 153, 159, 160
Cicero, M. Tullius, 48, 89, 106, 114, 117, 119 ff., 145
Citizenship, 86 ff., 99, 144
Claudius, Emperor, 133, 142, 150, 155
Colonies, 28, 33, 66
Commercium, 22, 27
Constantine, Emperor, 162

Consuls, 21, 48 ff., 128
Corfinium, 100

Education, 41, 79, 153
Etruscans, the, 15 ff., 20 ff., 31, 60

Familia, 38 ff., 78
Flaminius, Gaius, 66 ff.
Fregellae, 33
Frontiers, 108, 111, 130, 132 ff., 151, 152, 155

Gauls, 24, 25, 31, 57, 64, 65, 109 ff.
Gilds under Empire, 145
Gracchus, Gaius, 89, 92–6, 110, 113, 115, 136
   Tiberius, 89–92, 99, 115

Hadrian, Emperor, 152–9
Hamilcar Barca, 61 ff.
Hannibal, 62 ff., 74, 84, 87
Hasdrubal, 69–71
Horace (*Odes*), 61, 136

Imperium, 44 ff., 48 ff., 84, 85, 130, 134
Inscriptions, 143

Julius Caesar, 9, 14, 89, 92, 98, 105, 109 ff., 122–4, 130, 136, 138, 149, 155, 157, 162
Jupiter, 20
Justinian, Emperor, 158

Latins, 17, 22 ff., 27, 28, 87
Law, Roman, 22, 52, 103, 157, 158, 163
Lives (Plutarch), 10, 11, 93, 95, 144
Livy, 26, 136

167

Lucretius, 106, 117, 118
Lucullus, L. Licinius, 107, 108
Lugdunum (Lyons), 132, 142

Macedon, 74, 75
Magistrates, 44–50
Marcus Aurelius, Emperor, 160–2
Marius, Gaius, 89, 96–8, 100, 101, 109
Massilia, 76, 141
Messana, 59, 60
Metaurus, battle of, 70
Mithradates, 106–8

Nero, C. Claudius, 70
Nero, Emperor, 150, 152
Nîmes (Nemausus), 141–2, 148, 158
Nobilis, 53

Odes (Horace), 61, 136

Paterfamilias, 40
Patricians, 50 ff.
Paul, St., 140, 141, 150
Pharsalia, battle of, 114
Philip of Macedon, 74, 85
Plebeians, 50 ff.
Pliny the Younger, 153, 154
Plutarch (Lives), 10, 11, 93, 95, 144
Pompey (Gnaeus Pompeius), 98, 107 ff., 131, 138
Pontifices, 45
Princeps, 128, 134, 135, 151
Provinces, 75, 108, 139–48, 152
Punic War, the Second, 60–72
Pyrrhus, 34 ff., 57

Regulus, M. Atilius, 61
Respublica, 48, 50, 128
Roma, the goddess, 132
Roman Walls (in Britain), 156

Samnites, 17, 29 ff., 68
Scipio Africanus, 64, 71
Senate, the, 21, 31, 34, 36, 42, 46, 49 ff., 60, 62, 67, 73, 74, 77, 84–6, 91, 94, 99, 103, 107, 109, 113, 114, 128, 130, 151
Sicily, 57, 58, 61, 64
  Greeks in, 57
Slavery, 82 ff., 92, 115, 145, 159
Spain, 64, 68, 69, 72, 113, 140
State, the Roman, 42–55
Stoic philosophy, the, 159, 160
Sulla, L. Cornelius, 96, 98, 100–6, 112, 124, 130

Tacitus, 10, 12, 52, 150
Tarentum, 34, 35
Tiber, River, 16, 17, 20, 23, 24
Tiberius, Emperor, 111, 112, 133, 134, 135, 136, 150
Tigranes of Armenia, 106, 107, 138
Town life in Roman Empire, 138–48
Trajan, Emperor, 151 ff.
Trasimene, battle of, 66
Tribunes of the people, 51, 91

Umbrians, 17

Verus, Lucius, 161
Veii, 23, 24
Veto, 49, 54, 91
Via Appia, 33
Via Flaminia, 33
Via Latina, 33
Virgil, 9, 10, 12, 122 ff., 129, 136

Zama, battle of, 71

Printed in Great Britain by Neill & Co. Ltd., Edinburgh

3·65